Get out of debt fast!

Peter Bassett F.R.A.S.

Further paperback copies and an e-book version with direct internet links can be purchased from…

www.outerspacebooks.com

Chapter	Name	Page

Section One

Getting your own back in the world of Credit...

Peter Bassett FRAS

I0485513

Take advantage of the banking system and set yourself free...

It is legal too!

Chapter 1   Introduction & Morale

Millions of people are struggling with debts today (9 million in the UK alone). It is easy to get caught in the trap of mounting bills & debts, but extremely difficult to get out. Some feel so trapped that they sadly take their own lives. Advice from banks can make matters worse. From personal experience of owing seven times what we were earning after tax to virtually paying it all off in just seven years, we have produced a book to help others find a painless way out in very easy steps without turning to Rocket Science; (teaching Rocket Science is my main business by the way).

The coronavirus outbreak has changed many people's lives and a wide variety of scenes. This book is not about microbiology or politics, but can help with improving finances. If only the reader learns a few tips, then the purchase has paid for itself perhaps a hundred times over.

In 2000, I only owed £12,000 on a mortgage, by 2003, with just one house move, home improvements and unexpected but essential purchases for my business, the debts shot up to over £128,000. At the worst possible moment our clients, nationally, slowed down payments to contractors due to a major audit that lasted three months; a major cash flow problem that I never experienced before. The debts climbed to £142,000.

It resulted in countless family arguments, hidden bills and embarrassing phone calls from banks and credit card companies. It caused many sleepless nights. After three years of surviving each bill demand, on one particular day in March 2006, I returned home, had dinner and felt unwell. I went to bed early and collapsed. The accumulated physical and mental stress took its toll and my body shut down. The only sense I had left was my hearing. Within minutes, paramedics surrounded me. This was the turning point when I knew I had to regain control. It did not even require sacrificing all holidays or reading books by candlelight in the freezing cold.

Around 80% of people deeply in debt never seek help (as I did not). This is often down to personal pride, embarrassment, or just a non-acceptance that there is a problem. With this book, you can remain discreet with your personal situation, and you can solve it for a very modest price. No other charges, no catch, no posh people in elegant offices (paid for by others in debt) trying to take advantage of your situation.

I have written this book to be as flexible as possible. In addition, there is a strong need to change spending habits to avoid the same problem recurring in the future. There are three main approaches that you can choose from;

1) Consolidate all your debts together with one single loan. Then increase your savings to reduce your worry and need for further credit. In the majority of cases, (70%) many will not change their spending habits and will rack up further debt in the future and not be too concerned about paying off the initial consolidated loan.

2) Consolidate all your debts together with one single loan. Then pay everything you can on it to reduce the interest burden. Reducing expenditure & increasing your income a little will be the concern of Section 2 & 3 of this book.

3) Play the finance market cleverly and clear your debts in a faster & cheaper way. This method will also give you the opportunity to regain some of your losses up to this point and get into new spending / investing habits to keep you out of any further debt in the future. This is the method I have used and developed over time.

There are several financial models that can be used, but by analysing figures only, my third suggested method is the fastest. Well you could win the lottery, but I certainly cannot guarantee it. If you do, I am your best friend.

It is possible that if this technique is popularised too much, then some financial institutions will change their rules to reduce the trend. In the meantime, just use the legal loop holes to get your finances back on track. Good luck!

Banks never seem to learn

My main motivation for writing this book is the disgust I feel toward financial institutions that still today give poor advice to gain commission on products they sell without the slightest remorse.

Even my own Mother was advised by Halifax Bank in 2010 to invest all her savings on the Stock Market in a long-term contract; she was 78 at the time. She trusted people in expensive suits, posh offices and a free cup of tea. She just signed.

Nat West Bank advised me in 2011 to covert a zero percent credit card debt of £6,200 fixed for 14 months to a loan of 18% over 5 years; I did not sign. I failed my O' Level maths at school twice but I do realise 0% is less than 18%. They just do not stop.

My Mother-in-law found an old Woolwich Bank Account with a £1,800 balance. Barclays Bank bought up the Woolwich in 2005, they found details of her old account but claim she must have closed it and withdrawn all the funds. Her particular account would not allow such a transaction without it being entered in her passbook; it wasn't'. However, Barclay's have stuck to their story and she lost £1,800. Even the UK Bank Ombudsman could not take the case any further.

Northern Rock used to charge me a PPI cover even though I was self employed. When I tried to claim it back, they just said they could not find my records; I gave them statements, copy of the policy etc but to them it was not enough.

These are all forms of theft or attempted theft. When a hungry member of the public steals an apple from a store, the police are called in. When a financial body steals billions of pounds from the public and are found out; they are rewarded with money from taxpayers.

They have not learnt anything from the revealed bank frauds, but just continue on using different tactics and loopholes in banking rules instead. The staff behind the counters are mostly nice people scratching a living as with the rest of us, but these so-called finance experts are rouge traders in disguise.

They have no remorse, nor should you when it comes to clearing your debts.

Other Bank Swindles...

We now hear of Interest Rate Fixing, poor advice on the best type of Account to operate with thrown in holiday insurance that is not worth the paper it is written on, mobile phone insurance for a phone that maybe worth £10. RBS have even put perfectly well run and profitable companies in such a difficult position that they end up selling to out to a company related to RBS so they can grab the assets. The appalling list expands by the month.

So far the banks have cost Britain £10 trillion through greedy traders since 2008; as great a sum as the cost of World War Two at today's' value. Please do not feel guilty about the banks losing money as you pay back your liabilities.

December 2015, Lloyds Bank in the UK commenced showing a TV commercial of a child buying a star. As an Astronomer, I can assure everyone that such services are never official; the company taking your money only recognises the named star. So not only have banks ripped off customers, they are now promoting companies that offer rip- off services too. I did write to Lloyds about this matter and received a reply admitting that the Star Naming Services are not official and '*can be classed as a scam.*' I am keeping the letter in case of any feedback from the bank regarding this book.

Fast Start

A rapid start can make you feel more at ease within hours of purchasing this book. So much can be arranged on the internet without bad advice from 'experts' hampering your efforts. If you are not online, please do approach a trusting friend who is to help you. Each chapter will take that into account.

This book is <u>not</u> about giving investment advice, but how to reduce your debts quickly and get back a much more rewarding life without hiding your mail and dreading phone calls etc. It is simplistic and straight to-the-point rather than waffling on page after page about one small issue to save 50p, or giving a rundown of my life story that would bore the pants off you. As time ticks by, interest is pilling up by the day literally. If I waste one day of time, it will cost you tens of pounds / dollars.

The chapters are listed in a rough order of importance. If you have a mixed debt situation, then the order at which they should be tackled is as suggested here. Time consumption against potential gain was my reason behind the order of listing. I do realise that everyone's situation is different.

This is written for the UK market, but the principles are the same globally. Some advisors recommend that you should just pay the minimum off your debts and build up savings instead. However, the debts will not vanish; they will accumulate a higher interest charge for years. You may feel a little better with an increasing rainy day fund, but the debts will remain taking even more of your finite time on this earth to pay it off.

The End of Great Britain?

It is very possible that another deep financial crisis is looming ahead for the UK and USA. The UK personal + state debt as of November 2020 was £1,907,000,000,000: during this current updated book of May 2025, it's now £3.167 trillion and rising at

£3000 a second. This is clearly unsustainable for such a small nation.

The USA national debt was over $26,000,000,000,000 in 2020; in 2025 it's now $36.2 trillion. It is still increasing by a further $2 trillion a year even under normal circumstances. The only way to discourage further borrowing by Government & Individuals is to raise Interest Rates.

UK public sector net debt

Excluding public sector banks

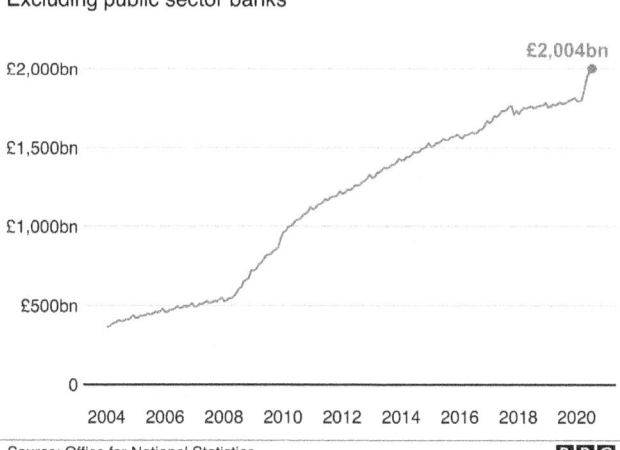

Source: Office for National Statistics   BBC

From 2014, statistics show that the UK entered a steady rate of economic growth. What is never shown is how much total extra credit exists in the same period; this should be subtracted from the growth. They say government borrowing is down; what does that mean? It just means they are not borrowing as much per day as they were this time last year. The overall debt is still increasing. They just play around with figures until they sound positive after baffling everyone. The Coronavirus crisis altered the figures drastically for the worse. After the crisis, most of this debt was swept under the carpet. As from 2024, the newly elected Labour Government as at least admitted to the problem and made drastic decisions on how to tackle it. We all need to prepare for increased taxes and reduced services.

As my own business is based around a school service, it has been hit hard. My bookings have more than halved and is unsustainable. I decided to semi retire and make some large decisions to make it happen. More detail later.

Going back to December 2015, an announcement was made in the press that the UK recovery seems to be slowing as personal credit is being stretched to its limit... as predicted by little me. Economics is not rocket science. Ignore personal feelings, observe the numbers and especially define the source of the information.

Another crucial point, in 2012, the UK Government spent an extra £120 billion more than it collected in tax. They had to keep interest rates low ever since, as they cannot even afford to make higher repayments themselves. To solve the borrowing habit from the public, taxes would have to be raised substantially or massive cuts in spending; far more than seem to have happened already. This will inevitably lose millions of votes in future elections; so the problem is never addressed. It is just hid within lots of percentage figures that sound as if they know what they are talking about and it is all under control. This has been an ongoing trend for many years.

Individuals already owing large sums of money will be heading for a big shock indeed. As an interest rate rise to discourage credit spending will affect voters, they are delaying the inevitable as long as possible; but it will only make the long-term problem worse.

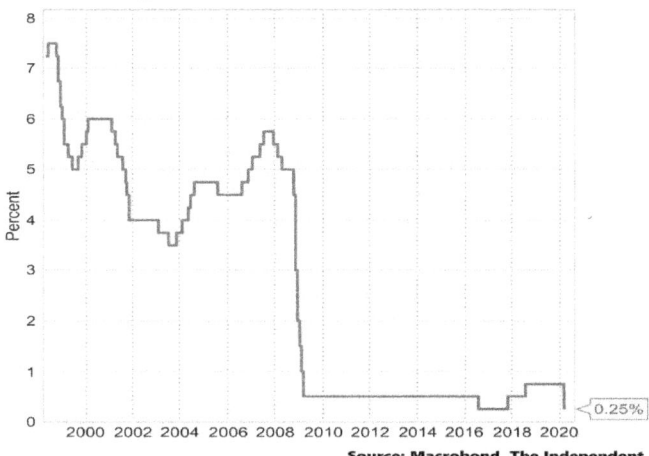

Bank of England interest rate

Source: Macrobond, The Independent

As the interest rate remains low, the incentive to save is almost non-existent too. People are spending more from savings or on cheap credit, building up personal debt even further. It does make the economy sound healthier for a time, but if it is largely built on spending past savings or on new credit, then it is a false reality. Savings will always run dry, credit limits will be reached; a massive depression is almost inevitable. The sooner individuals' act now and get finances in order, the safer each person will be. Those that do not act at all will be affected the most. Bankruptcy could become our national pastime.

As of January 2015, with the crash of the oil price, North Sea oil for the UK has almost become too expensive to extract. Thousands of people have already been laid off and re-investment became almost non-existent. It will soon be cheaper to leave it in the ground. Where would such energy come from then? Imported off course. Our dependence on the rest of the world supplying us with energy for transport and electricity becomes complete. Experts in the market feel that low oil prices could continue until around 2021.

The EU have officially entered a period of negative inflation. Prices are falling across most markets. This is the first time it has happened in EU history. The UK is about to follow. Our politicians tell us *'Don't worry about it.'* That is when I worry.

Japan had the same experience and the economy flat-lined for 10 years. No nation wanted to invest in Japan due to such figures and the Japanese public did not want to spend either.

We cannot sort out the national debt with this small book, but we can solve our personal debts. If millions of people did this at once, then the biggest possible collapse in UK history could be avoided. I hope this book will help at least a little. This is my personal goal.

April 2020
Regarding the behaviour of banks during the Coronavirus crisis, they have performed remarkably well. Some offered free £500 overdraughts, mortgage holidays etc. without penalties or affecting credit scores. Many of these offers were voluntary in advance of a government response. This is a very welcomed change in performance. Time will tell if this is a permanent change of heart or just a temporary glitch.

Morale
It is often said that the nation(s) with the highest morale will win a war. This has often been proved true. Propaganda became an important issue during World War 2 in particular.

Within a personal financial crisis, I have found that watching the news on a daily basis can become a depressing and sole destroying pastime. As recent as April 2020 at the beginning of the lock-down in the UK, I caught a glimpse of an apparently alarming report. It was something along the lines *'Here at Wakefield Hospital, 80% of the Accident & Emergency ward has been closed out of desperation and reserved for Covid 19 patients of the future. If you break your arm in an accident, don't come here; go to another hospital many more miles away.'*

Upon checking the hospital's website, another story emerged. From memory, it read *'Since the lock-down, the number of people arriving in our Accident & Emergency ward has reduced to 20% of our full capacity. Hardly anyone was coming in from road accidents, playground or work injuries, nobody was walking in with a nosebleed or a splinter in a finger type of*

12

incident. It made sense to convert 80% of the ward over to potential Covid 19 patients in the near future. Our A&E department will still accept cases as normal.'

The total number of deaths from the virus also included thousands of terminally ill patients with unrelated medical problems but caught the virus just before passing away.

These forms of miss-representation of facts continue in almost every form of news bulletin. They seem to gain pleasure out of depressing the audience. I choose not to watch it, or purchase any newspaper as a result. Euro News seems to be closest to a more neutral ground.

 My own father had on his own death certificate *'Pneumonia.'* Nothing was ever mentioned of his 50 years of smoking that brought on lung cancer and led to pneumonia. It is another example of twisting of facts.

Ask yourself, *'Can I control the world? Can I control the country? Can I control my town? Can I control my home?'* I hope that the last question will be answered *'Yes.'* Concentrate on that one issue and ignore everything else. Watching the news will not help your situation. If you need a specific item such as a new benefit, potential grant, interest rate change etc., these facts can be sought without watching any form of news, or at least be very careful about interpretation.

Perhaps a reader may not take on all of the points mentioned in this publication, but even if some saved a £1000 in unnecessary expense, then this purchase has paid for itself over a hundred times: £1 out, over £100 back. What investment could do better? The finest investment anyone can make is in yourself.

Chapter 2   Good Debts / Bad Debts

Good Debts

Some debts that may have accrued over time are necessary. It is often pointless to save for something and end up paying a lot more for the same later. I once had the opportunity to purchase a document hand written by John F. Kennedy for £800. I should have got out a credit card and purchased it right there with a trembling hand. I tried to save for a similar item at a later date and discovered that it had risen in value to over £4000. It would have been far better to have stuck to the numbers rather than be scared by the interest I would have paid. Since then I have slowly trained my feeble brain to stick to the figures only and ignore my stupid feelings. Today the same kind of investment would have been valued at around £10,000. It was one of my biggest financial regrets.

To save for a house and pay in cash is not often practical either. You may be able to save say £10,000 a year but it would still take say 15 years to save for a first apartment / home of £150,000. The pounds of interest gained may just cover the legal fees. During that period, the price may have increased by another £40,000. However, if you purchase via a deposit & mortgage, you effectively freeze the price and just pay back the debt. This is classed as a good debt. On the down side, the value of the property can reduce but this will only be noticed if you move; so do not move; improve the property instead. Interest rates will begin to rise at some point in the future, *batten down the hatches* for that one.

A private home is a long-term investment. Buying a home is not always a personal goal. There are advantages of being more mobile and rent instead. This book tries to consider such different priorities.

If you own your own property, then major improvements to it that increases the value and / or reduce household bills can also be classed as a good debt. However, be very careful about how much improvements really cost.

A 10x14ft conservatory for instance should only cost around £8000, but many companies often charge £12,000 for any conservatory. Do shop around; take no notice of any 'pep talk' to win you over. A Heat Pump (A refrigerator in reverse that compresses heat from outside to your home) should only cost around £650-£850 to purchase and three hours of work to install; just check ebay for such devices. Quotes are often given of £5000-£7000. This would clearly be a waste of money. Extra efficient double-glazing that may cost £6000 to save £200 a year on heating; a 30yr payback period is ridiculous. So do investigate the numbers properly independent of any hard sales pitch.

NEVER accept under any circumstance the phrase
'This offer is only available today!'

This is almost guaranteed to be a lie and be suspicious of any other claim from the entire conversation.

Further Education can be classed as a good debt also. If you are considering it and borrowing heavy to pay for it, please do look at the Open University options where you can still earn as you learn at home. The fees are greatly lower; a debt of tens of thousands will not be induced. Aside from that Apprenticeships are another example of earn as you learn with work experience included.

Starting a business may require a loan. When I started my business, I had to borrow £9,000 to top up my savings so I could start immediately. If I had waited and saved, then I would have missed out on a £5,500 voluntary redundancy offer, plus the market I was entering would have definitely accrued extra competition. Starting up would have been so much harder and more expensive. It would have cost far more than the interest I paid on repayments, and I would have spent one more year in a dull job. This was a good debt that I never regretted and did not have any other loans to worry over.

Such good debts are still debts though as they can hinder other aspects of your life. They are still a worry, a bind and need to be paid off as fast as possible. A loan for a business can be used to reduce a tax burden as well as a start or expansion but if anything went wrong, it can close a business too. I paid off my 5 yr loan in 2 years just in case an unexpected change in personal circumstances or the market I was trading in reduced my income to service it. Other debts could then creep in just to keep afloat. These become the bad debts.

Bad Debts

Generally, these debts have accrued by spending either on daily bills, as the money was not available at the time or just overspending on holidays, clothes, electronic gadgets, overpriced home improvements etc. For those that are in serious financial difficulty, a completely new way of looking at spending habits need to be developed. Once a full recovery has been made, thousands of pounds will be saved in the future as the new spending habits continue.

People can approach the Citizens Advice Bureau (UK). This can be a useful move for some. The staff are not on bonuses; the advice is not swayed toward keeping their own jobs or promotion. Some of their help can be a good move but they can only advise; put you in touch with an organisation, hand you leaflets etc that may then help directly. They will not actually do anything directly for you. You still have to make your own decisions.

Bankruptcy Option

This really would be the last option if your situation is totally out of control. But please study this book first. Your situation may not be as bad as you think. With Bankruptcy, you will lose all your assets, anything of value will be sold off until either all your debts are cleared or you run out of assets; whichever comes first. On the plus side, a line can now be drawn one year from the final solution date and it means a new start can be made with savings etc without creditors chasing after you. For those that have gone or going through this, then a lesson needs to be learnt so the same never happens again.

Many millionaires have experienced this and built a successful career regardless. They often use the thought of this past embarrassment / failure as a form of motivation to avoid the same ever happening again and then simply to try to make up for lost time.

Chapter 3   Preparation
Emotion

Take all emotion out of your decisions. Stick to the numbers only!

This is very important. Do refer to this point often to keep on track.

Examples...

You have a flashy looking credit card that is personalised with your choice of picture; ignore it. Study the Interest rate only and forget the picture.

There may be fun characters at your bank (or someone you fancy); they just want a share of your money. They will slow down your progress or even make it worse.

Totally ignore impressive easy money fun TV commercials; blank out the Payday loans at all costs. Look at the small print on the bottom of the screen - if you can, they tend to squash up the print so it becomes a blur.

It may sound posh to your friends to go to your bank or a specialised finance advisor for help, do not go there. They will take advantage of you and take another portion of your money that you could have put on your debts instead.

A friend of many years may recommend a product or course of action. Research it by all means, but make up your own mind coldly later.

Ignore friendly *'advice'* from any financial institutions via the phone. They do not know your full circumstances through a phone call from India. They could not care less about really helping you, just concerned about their own commission.

A friendly sales pitch by someone trying to sell you a special form of environmentally efficient Heat Pump for £7000 to save you £200 on your heating bill. Under perfect weather and home insulation conditions, it will still take 35 years just to get your money back, providing you do not move or die in the meantime.

If you research this fully, you will find the same product on ebay for £650-£850. Just call around to get someone to fit it. They only take around 2hrs to install. You should only need to pay £1000 not £7000. By saving £200 a year on heating, it will only now take 5 years to gain a return on your investment.

Walk away from ALL sales pitches and work out the numbers yourself. Above all, ignore special offers where they claim is only available that day. They know you can carry out your own research and discover the lies!

Do you see the point here? Numbers are very simple to calculate, but the emotion side is understandably hard to ignore. Sales experts know this and use it to their advantage. This one single action on your part can save you thousands of pounds in future debts / expenditures. This is the first step in regaining control.

Now list your debts

All you really need is to do first is to gather your figures of what you owe, to whom at what interest rate and minimum repayment per month. Shut out the fear of listing them. Be honest with yourself. Do not leave anything out. Do that first.

Example of listing...

Payday Loan;	£600 at 4,700%	£80 a month
Barclays Overdraft;	£718 at 16.5%	--------
Tesco Credit Card	£1,340 at 18.5%	£28 a month
Barclays Credit Card;	£8,280 at 19%	£64 a month
Virgin Credit Card;	£12,125 at 16.9%	£122 a month
Post Office Credit Card	£6,750 at 12.9%	£65 a month
Nat West Loan;	£9,600 at 15.9%	£340 a month
Lloyds Mortgage	£104,000ish at 2.99%	£780 a month
Minimum Total £ =	£143,413	£1,479 a month

(My own table like this was over £142,000 and required a minimum of £2,480 a month in 2006, more than what I was earning after tax and basic living expenses; as of 2015, its now zero).

Adding your Debts together – Consolidating

It may seem to make sense to consolidate all of these debts in one big new loan. The total repayment each month will be much lower than £1,479 a month, but you will be stuck on one interest rate that cannot be moved. The amount owed will remain the same. In addition, without getting out of the spending habit first, most people making such a move will not make any extra payments on the loan with the spare money each month. The spending almost always increases instead. This is what a lender is relying on.

However, if you really feel that consolidating your debts to one big one is just right for you, then please do put ALL of the spare money you now have each month as extra payments, change your spending habits at the same time, and skip to Part 2 of this book. Also, search for the best deal and do not secure it against your home if you own one. Without this extra action, your situation

20

could get worse in the longer term. *The total interest payable by completion will be far higher and take longer to payback than the method shown in Part 1 of this book.*

Produce a filling system of your creditors.

Keep all the statements tidy; know when each bill is due.

Produce a table of dates on a white board or put them on a calendar.

Never be late for a payment, this will incur extra costs and damage your credit score that will hinder your future efforts.

It is even worth withdrawing some funds from one credit card to pay another in the early stages just to reduce unpaid bills ready for the next phase. Only do this for a month or two. After this period other funds should be available to get you back on track if ideas presented later in this book is adhered to.

Chapter 4   Is combining debts good for you?

Some financial advisors will try to tempt you into listing all your debts and paying them all off from one single loan. This can make sense for some. If you are not good at record keeping and just want to simplify your situation this may be for you. At the same time, you must remember that the loan will almost certainly be over a long period of time; 10 years or more. The accumulated interest over the total repayment period will be far higher than my method described from Chapter 5 to 12. This is my main concern. Secondly, the spending habit that accumulated the debt in the first instance has not been addressed. A second wave of debt usually recurs unless Sections Two & Three are adopted in full. (Refer to Chapter 5 & 6 too).

There are two approaches here;

A) Consolidate your debts and raise savings to reduce the need for further debt;

B) Consolidate your debts then ignore savings, just cut your loan by making extra payments as often as you can. This will save you money. You choose at the end of the day.

A few points to remember

1) Search widely for the best interest rate. If you have a poor credit score at this stage, you may not get a good rate anywhere.

2) Don't choose too short a term for the opening loan. It can be shortened later with extra payments if you decide on option B. This may help secure a slightly lower interest rate too. A longer-term loan will allow a smaller minimum payment that may be much easier for you to manage without any further borrowing. Most lenders will not penalise you if extra repayments are made but do ask openly about it. Ask for the relevant small print in the contract before you sign.

3) Your course of action from this point is to free up every spare penny you can make available to make extra payments. Start from day one! On a 10-year agreement; if you managed to pay double for the first 7 months or so then a whole year is taken off the full term.

As soon as you get home, begin the Super Scrimping Section 2 of this book. Also, concern yourself with your Direct Debits as mentioned in Chapter 5 as well as a progress table in Chapter 6.

Write a standard letter as suggested in this chapter and print out many copies. Hand write in the figure you have spare to pay extra on the day. Ask for a receipt for that extra payment and file it away. When you get your annual statement, check every entry corresponding with your records of payments. Do not let them get away with a single missing entry. You have the receipts to prove your side. Get it corrected and the corresponding interest taken off the balance. Show no remorse, as they will not.

Even if you only have £20 spare to put on a £30,000 loan for example, do not feel bashful about it. The cashier may smirk secretly at your effort, but you have just stopped the interest from being charged from that £20 for the entire duration of the loan. This could save you another £10 or more in future interest. So have a smirk at them as you walk out the door. Begin planning your next extra payment straight away. If you do not have this approach, they have won again.

Mrs A Smith
32 Mug No More Street
Debt Crushing Town
Surrey SM32 4GG

01234 567890

07 May 2025

Loan Account No 01 2345 6789

Barclays Bank,
               Could you please accept the payment of £......as an extra deposit for the above mentioned loan?

I would be grateful for a receipt of this transaction.

Many thanks,

Signed ....

Type up a standard letter such as this and produce many copies. All that is then required is to fill in the two blank spaces each time you go into the bank. Insist on a receipt and keep it in a file. They can easily claim not have a record of a transaction, but you have. They are hoping you are untidy and have no proof. It is more common than you may think. They will try everything to take more of your money.

Important; One further piece of advice with this method of consolidation, reduce your outgoing monies rapidly and ensure all your bills are paid fully and on time for 3 months first. This will raise your credit rating and hopefully gain a better deal regarding the interest rate of your new loan. This will be fixed according to your credit report at the time of application only. It will not be reduced during the repayment period even though your credit score may continue to rise. The only way of taking advantage of that possible situation is to move the loan to yet another bank a year or so later; this may incur charges but shop around to make the move worthwhile.

Debt Advisory Companies

Some companies such as the Debt Advisory Centre UK (www.debtadvisorycentre.co.uk) can negotiate your debts with all your creditors and request a lower interest / repayment rate. They will charge a fee that is connected with your savings that can run into thousands by the end of your term. In addition, your credit score will be seriously affected and reduce your chances of obtaining a new mortgage for instance for many years. It may be suitable for some people in extreme cases. Be very careful with the small print, it is incredibly complex regarding fees. A late payment for a credit card will only affect your credit score for a couple of months. All three methods mentioned in this book will *increase* your credit score in the short and long term.

Chapter 5   Order of Priority

Step One; Direct Debits

Take a glance at the last three months of bank statements. Study every single Direct Debit and understand what they are all for. Ask yourself honestly: are there are any unnecessary debits? You may have insurances that are useless to you. I found two straightaways. Write to the bank with your account number and ask them to be stopped. This can be done online too to save time, a postage stamp or embarrassment. Some insurance policies can be partly reclaimed. Each day wasted in <u>not</u> doing this will take you closer to the next unrecoverable payment. Do this now!

There may even be a charitable donation you make. Find out how much of really goes to the charity. Many will only actually receive a small percentage of the total. Stop the direct debit and pay the charity the remainder direct to them. Many of them have to pay up to 60% of all their donations to a Limited company that raises them permanently rather than a one-off fee.

If your situation is dire, consider stopping the donations for two years. After which you should be in a position to restart them but with a larger sum instead as your finances should look much healthier. The charity will benefit more from you in the longer term.

If a particular service such as an Internet Broadband + TV + Phone package has increased recently, give the account department a call and ask them to drop the package to a cheaper deal with fewer services. In almost every case, they will agree to drop your direct debit by a few pounds / dollars instead. We do this every other year and we have never had a withdrawn or slower service.

Please act on this now before you go any further. Make a list of the Direct Debits you feel you can stop. Next; go online and stop them or write a letter with the details and give it to your bank within hours of reading this. A one-day delay will take you closer to the next payment.

Step Two; List

The order of dealing with each debt depends on the interest rate. Obviously, on the example list in Chapter 3, the Payday loan is by far the worst. This loan could go on for years. I would phone them, ask for the outstanding balance for say in 5 working days time and set the date. Find the lowest Credit Card percentage rate you have, in this case the Post Office. Arrange for the equal amount of money to be transferred into your bank account, no more. Once it has cleared, phone the Payday lender on the 5th day as requested and pay it off in full from your bank account immediately. Once that debt bites the dust; the £80 a month you were paying to the payday loan can now be transferred to your other debts instead.

Obviously, your debt on the Post Office card has increased but your total repayment time and interest rate has greatly reduced already. The minimum total repayments have now reduced by around £55 but do pay the £55 saved on top of the next most expensive debt instead; it probably will still be the Post Office Card anyway as your £600 transfer is classed as Cash rather than a purchase; but a possible 25% interest charge is rather lower than thousands. This part of the debt will be repaid first as the all credit cards now have to address the most expensive debt portion first, (it used to be at their discretion; the lowest part first while the more expensive part builds up and up compounding the interest for months or even years).

Another bonus from this one single action; as you have paid off a loan early, your credit score should rise. They do not know how you did it, your total debt has not reduced but that does not matter. It shows credit agencies that you are taking steps to deal with your situation rather than letting it control you. Other cheaper credit offers could now start landing on your doorstep.

Step Three; The credit card shuffle

Credit Card Balance Transfer offers are the key to the next phase. They all offer them as they hope that you will still owe them thousands by the time the offer ends and you continue overspending. There is a small fee for each transfer, but this disadvantage still far lower than the massive advantage of an interest free loan. When you now make repayments on the card, the most expensive part of the card debt is repaid first. If all of the balance is a transfer, then every penny you pay each month is a penny off what is owed.

Full details on taking the best advantage of this is given in Chapter 9.

Step Four; Addressing Loans

Once all the credit card debt is on 0% interest, pay twice the minimum payment each month if you can. If you only pay the minimum, the credit cards will think you are struggling and will lower your credit score. Less 0%, offers will be made to you and any other form of credit for the future will be offered at a much higher percentage rate.

The remaining money that you should have spare each month ought to be used as extra payments on loans not credit cards. Each pound extra paid off is another pound you are not paying interest on for the entire period of that loan. Loans are more restricting than credit cards as each monthly demand is a fixed amount weather you can afford it or not. This is the fastest way of increasing your overdraft debt. So get shot of loans first. Credit cards later. Loans can also be transferred over to a credit card, more details in Chapter 8.

Use the tips and standard extra repayment letter as described in Chapter 4.

Step Five; Household Bills

Address your household bills. Each is studied in more detail in Section 2. Reducing your monthly bills for Electricity, Internet service etc will free up even more funds for repaying debts without working harder.

Step Six; Changing habits

During the handling of the previous recommended steps, re-adjust your spending habits on shopping, eating out, holidays etc. It is not a question of not going out anywhere or doing without any treats at all, but just a change in how you do it. The more cash that is freed up, the faster you can get this problem out of your life forever.

Chapter 6   Progress Table

To demonstrate how your efforts are making a difference, produce a simple table that shows month by month your outstanding balances and minimum payments. This should be referred to every time a payment is made. Re-calculating the totals will keep your chin up toward another payment. Do not worry about how long it may seem to take for everything to be paid off; ignore that completely for now. Just keep your eye on the totals. As long as they are going down, the process will accelerate and your motivation will improve to continue. The order of priority should be as mentioned in the previous chapter.

The left hand side should be a list of your creditors. Allow a column for your credit limits on your credit cards. Then a column is required for each month showing outstanding balances.

Expand the table as the months pass to monitor your progress...

Debt Source	Credit Limit	Jan	Feb	March	Min Payments	Interest Rate
Nat West Credit Card	£5,000	£3,900	£3,840	£3,790	£51	18 %
Virgin Credit Card	£12,800	£7,300	£7,200	£7,100	£100	0% until Aug
TSB Loan	-----	£6,490	£6,340	£6,190	£388	16%
Payday Loan	-----	£1500	£1,460	£1,420	£180	4,700%
Nat West Overdraft	£1,100	£910	£920	£880	----	18.9%
Tesco Credit Card	£6,000	£4,380	£4,310	£4,240	£58	0% until Apr next yr
TSB Credit Card	£8,500	£6,940	£6,810	£6,700	£130	16.9%
Mortgage	----	£88,300	£87,900	£87,500	£785	3.99%
Totals	£38,400	£119,720	£118,780	£117,840	£1,692	
Paid Off	---	---	£940	£960		11 yrs payback

As you can see from this example a slow recovery is being made. At this rate, it will take approximately 130 months to pay everything off or just under 11 yrs. £700 every month is wasted on interest alone. During that time your circumstances may change; a new baby, interest rate rise, health issues, losing a job etc. Just about anything can throw your plan off course.

Savings / Rainy day fund

If by any chance you have savings that you count as a 'Rainy Day Fund' for emergency car or home repairs etc, then think very carefully about it. All you really need is a zero-balance credit card instead.

Transfer the said savings onto your most tying debt(s). In the case shown here, it will be the Payday loan, secondly the TSB Loan. Give them a good bash instead of having savings for a rainy day.

You may suddenly need £300 for a crucial car repair, get out your zero-balance credit card. Four weeks later, you get the bill and will be given 18 days to pay it or so. That is 46 days to save £300 and pay it off. If you can only manage £200, you will only be charged around £2 interest on your next statement but you may have saved hundreds of pounds on future interest charges from your total debt. You can pay the minimum on the other credit cards for a while to help. You have not increased your total debts but you have accelerated your repayment plan. So please be careful about whether you really need a 'Rainy Day Fund.'

Think of the numbers only; ignore the worry!

Millionaires constantly think this way.

Revised Plan After a Credit Card Shuffle

Without increasing your income or selling anything, this is how the table should look after a few simple changes made by phone or online…

Debt Source	Credit Limit	April	May	June	Min Payments	Interest
Nat West Credit Card	£5,000	£4000	£3,900	£3,800	£47	0%
Virgin Credit Card	£12,800	£9,290	£9,190	£9,090	£100	0% until Aug
TSB Loan	-----	£5,850	£5,380	£4,865	£388	16%
Payday Loan	-----	£0	£0	£0	£0	4,700%
Nat West Overdraft	£1,100	£870	£830	£765	----	18.9%
Tesco Credit Card	£6,000	£5000	£4,900	£4,800	£58	0% until Apr next yr
TSB Credit Card	£8,500	£0	£0	£0	£0	0% until June next yr
Mortgage	----	£87,100	£86,700	£86,300	£785	3.99%
Sainsburys Credit Card	£5,000	£3,500	£3,400	£3,300	£50	0% until June next yr
Totals	£38,400	£115,610	£114,300	£112,920	£1,428	
Paid Off	---	---	*£1,310*	*£1,380*	---	7yr 6 month payback

In the second table, the Payday loan has been transferred over to the Virgin Card on a 0% offer. Other cards have had the balances swapped over to 0% offers. Never get too close to your limit. If you keep a responsible distance, the supplier can raise your limit later by a larger amount than if you went right up to the limit. This higher credit limit will allow you to use 0% offers in a bigger way in the future. Do not cut them up either; just put them away. You can simplify the process by adding two or three card debts to one. A new card was also applied for to allow balances to be transferred without going over the existing credit limit of the others.

If you have spare cards with no balance owing, study their standard interest rates and close down the most expensive one by writing in and asking politely to have it closed. This one action alone will raise your credit score immediately.

More precise details of how to take full advantage of 0% offers after taking into account the small charge associated with them are in Chapter 9 on Credit Cards.

The rate of repayments has now increased. The minimum demand for your cash has reduced by £264; less need to use an overdraft. The debts are being serviced faster than before. Transfer all the saving on minimum payments should now to the Loan. At this rate the 5-yr loan will be paid back in around 10 months from June. The £388 will no longer be required, but the interest free rates will be ending so begin the Credit Card Shuffle again. The money that was being paid on the loan can be transferred to the other debts. The current amount of interest now being paid is only around £425 instead of £700. Once the loan & overdraft have gone, this will come down to around £370 in just 15 months from the start. The new rate of repayment will get you debt free in around 7yrs 6months from the beginning of this example.

I still would not be happy with that. To cut this time shorter still, we need to address your other household / day-to-day expenditures. At least one more year can be taken off in this example. By reducing other bills and basically wasteful spending; more cash can be freed to accelerate the whole repayment process. Increasing income will do the same. If both methods are addressed then perhaps three years or more can be taken off. With this example, you would be debt free in around 4 years rather than 11 years if you just plodded along. Everyone is in a unique situation, this book can only generalise but the principle is the same for all. **No bank manager will ever advise this method.**

Chapter 7   Payday Loans

If you have done this "Aaaarrrrrr!", if you haven't "Phew!"

Adverts by Payday loans constantly tell us that there are no hidden charges and that we are in control. They remind us that with such loans we can pay them back early and avoid future interest. They can also be short-term loans such as four months. Well guess what? All loans are the same!

Lenders are not allowed to pile on charges that you are not told about in your contract, nor can they stop you from making extra payments or paying up early in full. If you are concerned about a possible penalty charge for early repayment and you have £400 left to pay off for example; then pay off £380 and let the last £20 + accrued interest to the day be paid through your normal method on the existing due date. Early repayment fees do not normally apply unless the lender is greedy.

A lender may say they only lend on a minimum contract of 12 months. That is fine but you are perfectly entitled to make extra payments so it can be paid back in four months if required regardless of the 12-month contract. You are perfectly entitled to do this by law. There may be a slightly higher interest penalty upon final payment but that still makes it far cheaper than any Payday lender.

Such companies also claim that many clients repay the loan in full ahead of schedule. What they do not tell you is that the majority of those customers simply transfer the debt to another creditor that is cheaper. The result is indeed the same claim but give the impression that using a Payday loan is a good move and most people are happy with them.

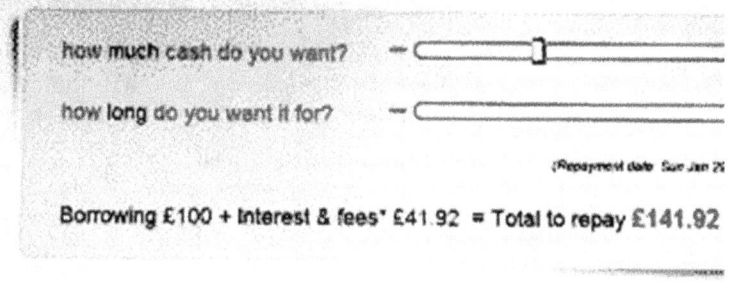

how much cash do you want?

how long do you want it for?

(Repayment date Sue Jan 29)

Borrowing £100 + Interest & fees* £41.92 = Total to repay £141.92

Representative APR 4214%

This example is for a Four Week loan of £100. An average credit card will charge around £2.80 + £2.50 perhaps for a cash withdrawal for the same deal, not £41.92. It is legalised theft!

Some Payday lenders may advertise that they are the fastest growing lender in the country – well they may have one customer on Jan 1st, five customers by Dec 31st. Therefore, they have expanded their customer base by 400% in one year. They are not lying are they? Many use this tactic. So be very careful about what any company may claim.

Luckily, for us, Martin Lewis approached the government about this very issue and many laws were changed regarding the method of how such companies can operate. Some payday loan companies now no longer exist, Wonga is one of them. Others still flout the regulations or at least push their operations to the upper legal limits.

If you have one or more of these loans, please do find a way of paying it / them off within days of reading this. Find out the balance you owe for a few days ahead and arrange other funds such as a credit card deposit to your bank and pay it off in full. Better still if you can, sell something of value that you really do not need; but try not to be forced into selling too cheaply. If you owe for example £1000 and you sell something for that then you not only save all those repayments, but also save on the future interest that would have pilled up. So by selling a personal item as in this example you are actually better off by say £2000 -

always include an estimate of future interest payments. Even paying off a portion would be a big help. Transfer the rest onto a credit card or similar. Preferably, transfer the whole balance first, the selling part second. Interest is charged daily. This is dealt with in more detail in Section 2 of this book.

You may be charged 30% interest after this suggested move from a loan to credit card, but that is rather lower than 4000% or more. Then you may have the opportunity to reduce it to 0%; more in chapter 9 on Credit Cards.

Once the loan/s has been cleared, your credit score will rise regardless of what it was before. Not because you owe less but because you have taken action to solve the worst part of your situation. This will help you request higher credit limits to cards if necessary for the next key steps in Chapter 8 & 9.

Chapter 8 Loans

Everybody is in a different situation. You may have no outstanding loans, if this is you then great; move on to the next chapter.

If you have one or more loans then these need to be dealt with immediately. The repayment date & amount are fixed whether you can afford it or not. If you do not have the required sum(s) ready in time you will almost certainly be using your overdraft, bounce the debit, or be creating a new or higher debt with your credit cards. I have been through it all. This is not a good situation to be in. You feel you have lost control and your creditors are in charge of your life. This obviously needs addressing fast. I have used two methods to paying off loans early.

Keeping the loan(s)

If you choose to keep your loans running to the bitter end, then do give this priority over credit cards. Through only paying the minimum on credit cards (or twice if you can to help your credit score; definitely no more) and through super scrimping described in Section Two, throw on as much money as you can. Make extra payments by using a simple letter as described in Chapter 4. Demand a receipt and keep it safe every time. Do not be shy about walking into your bank just to pay off £20 or so. From that day on, you will not be charged any interest on that sum. You are reducing the amount of money your creditor will take from you in the future. By law, it is recalculated daily. You are at least heading in the right direction. During this operation, move on fast to Chapter 9 on credit cards. This is the key to getting your life back. Every day you think about changing this or that will result in higher charges and the lenders win. Do not give them the satisfaction.

A radical idea

If you have sufficient credit limit left on a credit card to pay off a loan, then you may be advised to do this. Just call the creditor and find out the exact balance. You can make a transfer from your card into your bank account. Once cleared, recall the creditor of the loan, ask for the balance again to the penny and offer to repay it now. That Direct Debit will cease.

The interest rate on the card is normally higher than you were being charged on the loan but this can be solved in the next chapter. This will only be temporary. As a loan has been paid off early without applying for a new credit card it is often assumed by credit score agencies that your situation has improved and raise your credit score accordingly. This in turn will reward you with offers of 0% balance transfers within your existing cluster of credit cards. Transfer the balance of the whole card, if possible, to 0%. If you do not have many, then okay apply for a new one straight away. Almost all new customers will be offered a 0% transfer for at least 6 months. Even that will do for starters.

The biggest bonus from this move is that your minimum payments per month to service all your debts are now lower than before. This will reduce the chances of you not meeting future demands and help your credit score enormously. Do keep your repayments as high as before if you can, give priority to any remaining debts that attract interest and just service the rest to keep them happy.

This method may sound alarming to some, but I managed to clear two loans this way and transferred both extra debts on credit cards to 0% within four weeks. Both debts were paid off four months earlier than scheduled simply because every penny paid to the cards came off the debt not just 70% of it. It also allowed me to pay off a third loan nine months ahead of schedule because my minimum payments a month were reduced by over £400 and I threw that onto it. The choice is yours at the end of the day.

Chapter 9   Credit Cards

Many finance experts do advice cutting up credit cards and just concentrate in paying them off. I have found that credit cards can be used to your advantage in a massive way if you approach them with military precision. This is the key to paying off your debts faster than putting them all together in one massive loan or just servicing them till they all reach zero in your own time.

Personal financial situations constantly change from one month to the next, using credit cards will allow you to adjust the speed of repayments, a consolidating loan will not. If you cannot quite afford a loan payment for one month, you will have to borrow from elsewhere (open another new debt) to complete it or bounce the payment. The latter will add charges, lengthen your term or push up the monthly payment for the rest of the agreed term. It may even result in a higher interest charge, as you seem to be a higher risk than when the loan was taken out. They will say that you have broken the agreement. The small print will differ from one lender to another.

Store Cards

These often offer a 10% discount on everything you purchase on the day the card is applied for. This is a good idea especially if sales are on at the same time. Do not feel guilty. Then just do not use it. Any point system that may be associated with them are very poor and the interest charged is usually much higher than a normal credit card. Pay any balances on these cards off first or at least transfer the balance over to a 0% credit card offer straight away and cut up the store card.

Cash-back Cards

Some cards offer a cash sum every time it is used. You may be rewarded by 1-5% of everything you spend on it. It will not include balance transfers though. Such cards encourage spending on items that are not really needed just for the cash-back reward. Just do not get caught in this trap. If you spend a large amount on travel to work then this would be a great move. Purchase rail tickets, petrol etc on a cash-back card by all means as you were going to spend the same amount anyway. By the end of the year, you may have enough to purchase your Christmas Hamper for free. Always pay off the balance if Full every month – even just one- or two-months' worth of interest charge will wipe out any gain from the entire year. If you feel there is a big chance of not paying the balance in full then this is not for you.

Points Based Cards

Points systems such as Nectar is very tempting, every time you spend on your card, the more points you collect. To make it sound impressive each point has an extremely low true value. Such values vary from card to card. A Nectar point for example is worth just 0.5p. You may be tempted to purchase car insurance that offers 10,000 extra Nectar points via your card; it is worth £5. Big deal!

Each offer does vary; new ones start up every year. If you want to take advantage, do investigate the true value first. GM Card had a points offer – one point per £1 spent toward a brand-new Vauxhall car. As there was no limit as to the maximum points it was possible to buy the whole car on points alone. As some customers began to reach such a goal, the rules changed and then the offer was withdrawn.

0% Balance Transfer Offers

These are magic, gold dust; pennies from heaven, a fairy tale come true. This is the key to paying off your debts earlier than any consolidation loan. However, to make it work you need to be organised and totally dedicated to your goal of becoming debt free!

Letters like this one is what you pray for in the post. Applications can be made from scratch when applying for a new card but does affect your credit rating for a while. However, if you stay on track, pay twice the minimum every month then more will follow. It does not take long to see changes with your debt balance. The more of your debt that is passed onto such offers the better.

The 0% Magic Touch

If your limit is say £3,500; then do not transfer any more than 80% of that limit; £2,800. A charge of 2-4% will be incurred, but this will be made up within a few weeks of the transfer in saved interest. To tempt you into spending on your card, they will almost certainly contact you with a higher limit of perhaps £5,000. You will need this later for year two. If you transferred almost up to your limit, you may be offered an increase to around £3,900 or so instead. If you do not request a higher limit it sounds as if you do not need it, this will put you in a higher credit score for better offers later. Just be patient.

Each balance transfer has an associated charge. They vary from card to card from 2% to 4%; obviously the lower the better. Do not get too hung up on this, as your interest charge is zero then your savings will make up for this fee within 6-12 weeks. The rest of the time the offer runs for is your gain. For people with very good credit scores, they can be offered 0% balance transfers for up to 30 months.

Every penny you pay within the duration of this offer will come off what you owe. Do not be tempted to repay these 0% balances faster, the more money you can throw onto any loans instead the faster you will truly recover. Paying twice the minimum on the cards will suffice. If only the minimum is paid, then it will affect your credit score as it seems that you are struggling. Your interest free offers are <u>not</u> accumulating interest by the day, loans do. Concentrate on them at all costs.

Make a note of when each offer ends on your Progress Table as shown on Chapter 6. However, do not be tempted to increase payments on these cards, concentrate on loans. I cannot emphasise this enough. If you have no loans outstanding then great, pile it on as fast as you like on the lowest balance first. Once it gets close to zero, or even completely paid off, new 0% transfers will be offered. Discover the 0% card that is going to resort to full interest

next and transfer it to your new 0% offer. Keep thi
all your debts are completely cleared.

At this point, it is possible to slow down your repayme
2 x the minimum or so. As long as it is all on 0% inte
there is no hurry. The only problem is that other ur
factors may creep in; health issues, a new baby, job l
would be advisable therefore to play it safe and keep
payoff method working instead.

To sustain momentum, a Super scrimping policy is now
as mentioned in detail in Section Two of this book. The
to spend out so much, the more can be piled on to your
reduce the pressure to borrow more in the future. The
should become Zero as soon as possible. If you are
position that you need to borrow more at any time,
Section Two and Three as soon as you can.

Credit cards also usually have a low minimum
compared to a loan. They get smaller as the balance red
A loan will not. If you fancy giving your debt free plar
for a week or you perhaps have a lower income for a sho
then paying a smaller amount on a card is easy, but a loan
Usually loan repayments force people into borrowing
make a payment. So make sure loans dies first. Interest F
offers will increase as your extra payments on your loans
more common. This is due to your improving credit scor

The three main priorities should be;
1) Payday Loans
2) Ordinary Loans
3) Store & Credit Cards; aim to get it all on 0% o

This is defined by the interest rate & flexibility of pay
As I mentioned earlier, numbers are all we deal with

Chapter 10   Overdraft

An arranged bank overdraft is actually helpful. However, never go over the limit. The interest rate on an agreed limit is usually about the same as a credit card. As you make payments for loans and credit cards, if you do not have quite enough, then your overdraft will help keep that repayment momentum going; this helps to keep your credit score improving.

NEVER GO BEYOND YOUR ARRANGED LIMIT

The interest charged and extra-unarranged borrowing charges from the bank are usually huge. These can accumulate daily and many will not tell you for weeks. Some accounts now arrange a text to be sent to your phone if your account gets close to your limit. This is usually free. This one measure alone can save you hundreds of pounds.

As your outgoing funds decrease by following the method in this book, your need for an overdraft should reduce. If you are in the red, in time it will reduce and pass into the black. An overdraft debt in most cases is usually much smaller than loans or credit cards; more attention should be paid to them in the short term. An emergency cash withdrawal from a credit card and deposited in your account would be cheaper than exceeding your overdraft limit.

Paying money into your account is also best done via a machine, the 'Quick Deposit Box', or a machine in the bank itself. The cashier will always look at your statements as you pay in. He / she will often take that opportunity to see if they can 'help' by offering you yet another loan or replace existing loan(s) to a larger one to get your balance into the black. They do not know of your plan nor would they approve. So such potential conversations can be avoided by simply not going to the cashier in the first place.

Chapter 11   Mortgages

These are very complex products and are changing constantly. They can also take up to four months or so to transfer from an existing mortgage to a new one. It also arises in costs of hundreds of pounds in legal charges, commission fees etc. Sometimes it is best to keep an existing arrangement even though there may be a slightly better deal elsewhere. If an offer you see is much better than an existing one, then it will be worth investigating at least. To cover your costs, you need to have completed other sections of your plan so far mention in the book first and raise your credit score to get an even better deal (Chapter 12). If a mortgage is transferred first then vital funds, time and effort are being lost that could have had an immediate reward. Tackle the prior chapters first if you have not done so already and certainly <u>do not</u> consolidate all your debts into a new higher mortgage. If repayments fall behind, then you could lose your home.

As of April 2014, new rules regarding mortgages come into play. A more detailed analysis of your income and expenditures need to be gathered and submitted. Your potential lender will check many of these details. If every aspect of this book is addressed, you will be in a much better position to make such applications.

Chapter 12   Your Credit Score

There are several Credit Score companies that gather information about your credit history. This record of you changes every time you take out a loan, a new credit card, mortgage etc. In addition, your payment amount and regularity are also constantly assessed.

The rating scale is usually the same between them. It gives potential lenders an indication of your responsibility and ability to pay back credit. The higher the number (1-999) the lower perceived risk to the lender; therefore, you are more likely to be granted credit at better rates. If your score is low, then do not apply for any new credit cards just yet. Instead, make some extra payments on any loans you have and / or just ensure you pay twice the minimum credit card payment for a while. Then concentrate on Part 2 of this book in order to put more funds onto your loans first, then credit cards. You credit score will rise if you remain consistent. Part 3 will help raise extra funds for such payments.

One of the largest of such companies is Experian. (www.experian.co.uk). Sign up on their website and for a small fee you can gain access to this service. They usually offer a free introductory offer. You may be a little disappointed with your score and perhaps disheartened by it. Don't Panic! Once again, ignore your emotions and concentrate on the method of raising it. Cheaper credit offers will automatically follow. At my lowest point in 2006, my score was just 203, as of 2025, it's at 996.

If your score is very low, try applying for a high interest credit card. Aqua is one example. If accepted, use it for a few purchases you would normally have made in cash. Pay off the bill in full as soon as it comes in. This action alone will raise your credit score and zero percent offers will eventually appear through the post.

If you monitor your score regularly, you can time when it is best to apply for a new credit card, a 0% balance transfer etc. In addition, if anyone fraudulently applies for credit in your name, you will know about it. Checking your report will not affect your Credit Score in a negative way at all.

What your score means?

Category	Score range	Description
VERY POOR	0-560	Most lenders would regard this score as very high risk and would expect most people in this category to have serious problems with repaying credit.
POOR	561-720	Most lenders would view this score as high risk and would expect a high proportion of people in this category to have serious problems with repaying credit.
FAIR	721-880	Most lenders would regard this score as moderate risk and would expect only a small proportion of people in this category to experience serious problems with repaying credit.
GOOD	881-960	Most lenders would view this score as low risk and would expect few people in this category to experience serious problems with repaying credit.
EXCELLENT	961-999	Most lenders would regard this score as very low risk and would expect very few people in this category to experience serious problems with repaying credit.

My score...

When I first checked in 2006 it was 203; Very Poor. After ensuring all my payments were made on time and paying a little extra on the three loans and via super scrimping, the score raised to just over 400 within 10 weeks. As it was rapidly rising, the first 0% offer from a credit card for several years landed on my doorstep; that was even before I climbed out of the Very Poor credit class. I took advantage of it straight away. My first action was to transfer £2,100 from another credit card into my current account – ignoring advice from my bank who wanted me to take out a fourth loan. After clearing, I went into the same bank and paid off £2,135 for my smallest outstanding loan. With that cleared, I stopped paying the corresponding £122 a month. The credit card payments went up by just £35 a month but now paying a heavy 28% interest rate on that £2,100. Guess what I did next? I used the 0% offer on the other card for the completely new £6,200 balance. Normally such transactions attract a very low repayment figure to encourage you to owe more when the 0%

47

offer expires. Pay twice that minimum figure otherwise it will seem that you are struggling and will lower your credit score. The total result was a £50 a month reduction in outgoing funds, £20 a month saved on interest, plus a higher credit score.

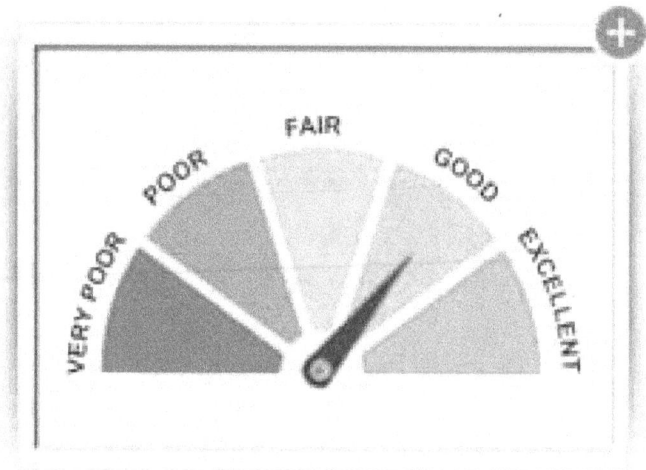

With one loan paid off early and one lower credit card payment demand, it was so much easier to find the money to make extra payments on two other loans while ensuring I paid double the minimum on the new 0% balance and also keep all the other cards happy. My credit score rose to over 600 in 10 more weeks. More 0% offers slapped on my doorstep. I began the process over again with a second loan. Do you see the principal? One part of the debt after another was being transferred onto a 0% credit card for 6 to 18 months as the credit score improved.

At all costs though, as you begin to feel wealthier, do not fall into the trap of rewarding yourself by going on a spending spree. Keep all your payments for day-to-day living an absolute minimum during the whole process. Reward yourself with zero cost days out. Take sandwiches, a flask of coffee; whatever you need to do and take a relaxing walk into the countryside. Just do not spend. Throw everything you can at these debts. As momentum increases (study you're Progress Chart), the more obsessed you should be with accelerating the process.

In just over seven years, I paid off £142,000. As of 2025, my score is 996 with mortgage paid off seven years early.

Once it crept down to a low enough level, I just transferred the remaining over to 0% credit cards to save the last few hundred pounds interest. It more than made up for the 2% balance transfer charge. Twelve months from that point, the remaining debt died. Debt free at last - all because I ignored advice from my bank and just studied the numbers. Since then we have invested in property in the USA and now concentrate on increasing its value.

Our Arizona investment –

www.northaroasis.co.uk

Section Two; Super Scrimping Big & Small

In order to accelerate your repayment plan, a Super Scrimping attitude will have to be developed if you have not already. Many people are doing just this in order to live more within their means and to be able to save for a rainy day. What most Super-scrimpers do not do though is factor in time. If it takes 2 hours to save £1, is your time worth more than 50p an hour? If it is then do not bother unless you want to for fun. Spend 10 minutes on the phone to arrange a 0% balance transfer and you may save £500 during the lifetime of that arrangement. That is equal to £3000 an hour; a gain of 6000x greater for your effort. This is precisely why I have arranged this book in such terms of priorities.

If you have completed the tasks in Section 1, then to sustain the momentum in paying everything off, this section also needs addressing. This should help to keep you on course and reduce the risk of re-entering the world of credit.

As addressed before, try not to let emotions get in your way. When I once sold a flash sports car for a rusty 16 yr old Datsun Cherry, I just concentrated on the numbers and kept a long awaited ambition to myself. I ended up touring 22 US states and driving 12,000 miles. I paid cash for it all. My 'mates' had the first laugh when they saw the rust bucket I was now driving, but I had the last laugh as I drove along The Strip at Las Vegas while they were delivering letters (I was a postman at the time).

If you have not yet tried the pound stores (Dollar General / Dollar Tree / Family Dollar in the US), then it is about time you did. Do not worry about your friends seeing you walking out of one. The harder you try to reduce your outgoing funds, the more can be poured onto the repayments. I do realise that some of their products are very poor quality but the vast majority are not.

Miscellaneous Examples.

Partying

If you want to hold a party, consider having an American style 'Pot Luck Party.' Everyone would be invited to bring a food & drink contribution and his or her own chair. All you need to supply are soft drinks and a few simple sandwiches. More socialising can happen this way without costing anything. Super scrimping is about living day to day differently rather than going without.

Phone calls

Even saving on phone calls can help. We are often offered a 0500, 0845 or 0870 numbers etc by banks and various companies. These are all charged calls regardless of what tariff you may be on. They play long-winded messages, then keep you on hold and hang up on you. You have to start all over. There is no incentive for the receiver to answer your query early. Forget this and try out www.saynoto0870.com . Just type in the charged number you are given and in most cases there is a 0800 free number or a landline number instead to the same department. Refuse to be ripped off in every aspect of your everyday living.

Going out

Checkout free days out such as parks, nature trails etc in your area. Take a packed lunch and prepared drinks. Having a treat while being in debt is good for your morale. Just do not spend anything, same with short breaks. Some hotels (Travelodge) offer £30 a night rooms if booked well in advance, off peak season. Such offers are usually for one night only. Just book 2 or 3 nights at the same place or another hotel nearby separately; we do that constantly.

Use a flask instead of coffee bars. If it saves you £80 a year, that is £80 off your debts and another £60 or so off any interest payments into the far future. Don't worry about what others think. (Do not mix in the milk until its poured; it will go off; serious tummy worries).

Chapter 13   The Gas Bill

Reducing the Gas bill is one of the hardest to address. As more natural gas is imported (concerning the UK market) the less control the UK has over its price. Demands cannot be placed on how other nations price their gas on the international market. The UK gas grid infrastructure desperately requires upgrading which costs billions too. If the UK companies had the selling price frozen as proposed by the Labour Party, then no extra money would be available for large-scale repairs, upgrading the grid or exploration and research. Outside companies would have no motivation to invest either. Even if the 'frozen price' policy held for two years or so, it would be a downward spiral to disaster. A massive price hike would follow to make up for lost time and investment.

'Fracking Gas' in the USA really has revolutionised their whole energy market; gas for heating, cooking and for electricity production has reduced dramatically helping the whole economy. It is still a fossil fuel that contributes to climate change and will not last forever. The same temporary opportunity will never be the same for the UK. The cost of the land, higher population density, protestors etc all add to the equation compared to the US example. It will probably never offer the same advantages despite what is heard on the news.

So what can we do to reduce our gas bills at home today? Here are some examples of changes that can be made to have an impact on your monthly demand. The more money saved on monthly bills, the more will be available to throw onto your debts.

Ensure you take a reading of your meter every month. If you get into the habit of doing this on the first, it is less likely that you will forget.

Phone in or fill in the meter reading form if you are registered online. This will help your supplier judge your Direct Debit more accurately. Once they have one year of constant readings, there is less of an excuse to overcharge you and pay the excess back months later. In the meantime, you have more money per month to slap on your debts.

If you are overcharged, most people are, you can request a monthly Direct Debit reduction.

Pressure Cookers & Steamers

Such devices are very cheap and last a long time. Replacement seals are required every two years or so and can be obtained easily. These require just one single ring on the stove to cook a whole meal for several people. This one change to cooking methods can lower a gas bill by a noticeable degree.

Slow Cookers

A fast way I found to deal with the gas bill is to convert some of your gas use over to efficient electric sources instead. A good quality slow cooker is a perfect start. It is Ideal for stews and casseroles, curries and even mulled wine.

On a slow setting, it may only require 50watts to operate; just 30% of the same cost with gas. At this level, there is the option of solar power at a later stage; zero cost energy. This part of your gas bill has reduced to zero regardless. (The potential of Solar Power is discussed briefly later; a separate book will be published in this series too).

They come in different volume sizes from 0.9 litres to 6 litres. Do not use one that is too big; waste power. Better still is to get perhaps two different sizes to perfectly suit any meal / sittings. Such a purchase will pay for itself within the first 18 meals or so. A 2.5lt cooker should not cost any more than £25 as a guide price.

Candles

Most of have candles been given as Christmas presents etc. Instead of turning on the central heating, burn a couple of candles with the doors closed and watch a movie while being cosy up on the sofa.

Thermostat

Simply turn down the thermostat by one degree or / and turn on the central heating an hour later than you normally would, turn it off an hour earlier. Just wrap up a little, you won't catch pneumonia.

Switching Supplier / Tariff...

Changing your supplier or tariff can save a little money on the first year or so. Overall British Gas has one of the most expensive tariffs on the UK market. Sales pitches always include 'We can guarantee to lower your Direct Debit by your existing supplier.' Yes they probably do. After a few months, you will receive a letter stating something like 'We now have a record of your consumption and have decided to raise your Direct Debit before you accumulate a large debt.'

Do use an energy supplier comparison website to ensure the best deal. Only so much can be achieved this way; saving on your consumption will drop down your bill regardless of what tariff you are on. With this method, you are in control rather than the confusing tariff system. So do investigate switching supplier followed by an energy efficiency drive around the home.

Be careful about how much the energy companies increase their prices each year and how you judge it. The starting points are different for each company. For example, British Gas may increase their price by 5% and another company 8%. However, if British Gas is charging 23p per kW and the other 18p per kW, then the other company is still cheaper after the price rise. British Gas will claim that their prices are not going up as much as others; that would be true. But the starting point is higher so still remain more expensive. Always be careful as to how the claim is worded. For several years we have used Octopus Energy.

Chapter 14   The Electricity Bill

Electric power consumption can be reduced more readily than gas. Some effort is required but you decide how far you want to go with this. Unlike saving on gas, there is literally no limit on this one. It is possible to reduce your electric bill to below zero; this is not a miss-print; as of 2019, our bill was around £2300 a year. After many more energy saving improvement, we have got it down to £1400 a year. Solar Power is the answer here. Unfortunately, the UK government has lost interest in giving incentives to expand this option as they claim it is too expensive to operate. They always fail to mention that the solar panels and wind farms in the UK now produce enough green energy that equals two nuclear power stations that would have cost £12 billion to build and around £60 billion to decommission at the end of their useful life. This is rarely factored in.

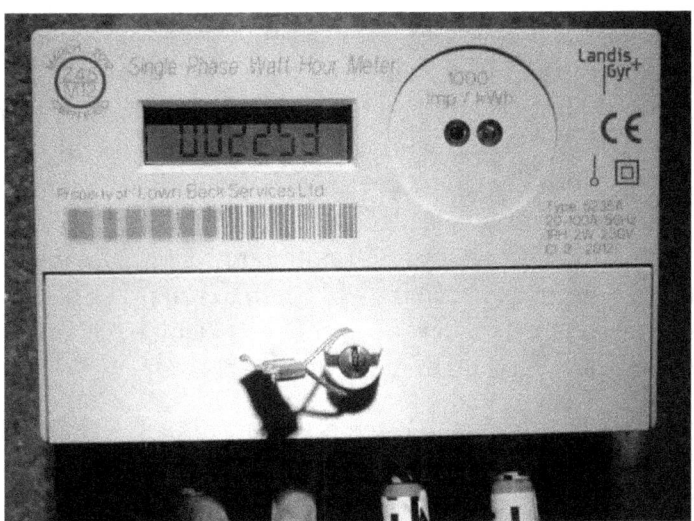

As with the gas bill, ensure you take a reading of your meter every month. If you get into the habit of doing this on the first of the month, it is less likely that you will forget.

Phone in or fill in the meter reading form if you are registered online. This will help your supplier judge your Direct Debit more accurately instead of guessing. Once they have one year of constant readings, there is less of an excuse to overcharge you and pay the excess back months later. In the meantime, you have more money per month to slap on your debts.

If you are overcharged, most people are, you can request a monthly Direct Debit reduction.

An energy monitor is very important. As you get to see your consumption live, it makes you aware of how much your property consumes. This knowledge alone should inspire to make savings; not by going without, but by handling your home differently. If you begin an energy efficiency drive, your efforts will be noticed on this gadget and then rewarded by a lower electricity bill. The savings will not be rewarded straight away, but as your electricity account will begin to run into a high credit figure, you can then request a lower Direct Debit from your bank. Extra funds are freed up to repay your debts.

The first generation 'Smart' meters that are already installed have a small glitch attached: they do not allow the user to change suppliers. If they do, the meter will no longer work. I am suspicious of every item or service that has the word 'smart' attached.

As you pop off to bed, ensure everything you can is switched off. The top figure on the unit will change within seconds of each action. Our consumption is less than 0.07kw by the time the last light goes out. Even though a monitor may cost around £30, it will pay for itself repeatedly in the first year alone.

Consider installing LED bulbs. They sound expensive at first but they cost 5% as much to run as Tungsten 30% in comparison to Compact Fluorescent bulbs. The potential is also there to convert your lights over to an independent Solar Power supply; i.e. not connected to the grid; free! We chose this method in 2020 and have never paid a penny to run the light circuit ever since.

Fridge Freezer

After heating, the biggest electricity cost for many households is refrigeration – because fridges and freezers need to be switched on around the clock. Research by 'Which?' magazine discovered that running costs for fridge-freezers could vary from £15 to £76 per year – with newer models generally being more efficient.

There is a slight problem with this policy. It may make perfect sense to ensure you have a low running cost freezer, but how is it achieved?

The key is in the insulation layers which reduces the overall capacity. If you there are more than two people in your household, it will almost certainly become a struggle to fit everything in. What happens next? Another freezer is purchased and the goal of reducing power consumption and saving money is lost. Any grade 'B' efficiency fridge-freezer will often have around 20% extra volume. The total annual cost will be lower than running two 'A' rated appliances.

However, if you already have an efficient appliance, cannot afford a new one or just want to economise further, there are a few simple tips you can follow: Let food cool down completely before you put it in the fridge or freezer, that way it does not have to work as hard to do its job. Make sure they are set to the correct temperature: go lower than 5C on your fridge or -18C on your freezer and you will be wasting energy. Shut the door in between taking items out and putting them back in. If defrosting food from the freezer, pop it in the fridge. This will cool things down in the fridge so it does not have to work so hard. Check that your refrigerator door shuts tightly - a door leak allows cool air to escape, forcing your refrigerator to use more energy to keep food cold. You may need to clean or replace the door seal. Automatic defrost refrigerators may be convenient but their defrosting features use much more electricity than a manual defrost model.

Electric hobs

Electric hobs might be easier to clean than their gas equivalents, but they also tend to cost twice as much to run because making heat from electricity is always a costly process. However, there are a few easy measures you can take every time you cook:

Keep the lid on when cooking; you will need less energy to heat your food. Cook food in large batches and keep in smaller portions, to be reheated when required. This will save time and energy. Only put enough water in the pan so that it just covers your vegetables. Use the microwave if you are just heating up some baked beans or reheating a dinner that has been cooked previously. Select the correct size of ring for your pan.

If buying new saucepans, copper-bottom ones conduct heat better than others and cast-iron pans retain it more effectively than stainless steel equivalents.

Televisions & Computer Monitors

The TV is the most energy-hungry entertainment appliance in the home according to the Energy Saving Trust. In addition, while larger sets are popular, they use more energy; for example, an A-rated 22" LCD TV might cost £6 a year to run compared to £31 for an A-rated 56" TV. When replacing a TV, always opt for an LED backlit model.

You can save energy by turning off the set when not using it, rather than leaving it on standby. In fact, simply turning off lights once you leave the room and not leaving appliances on standby could save the typical household between £50 and £90 per year.

Even if you only save a few pence a day, it can add up to big savings over the year. All such savings should be thrown onto your debts.

For desktop computers, do use the sleep button every time you walk away from it.

Kettles

Fill the cups you are going to use with cold water and tip it in the kettle to avoid over filling. Better still; try a model that has a 'cup indicator' and one that has no protruding heating element inside. The element has to be covered with water plus water that you need for your tea / coffee. This tip is mentioned repeatedly on TV, but few people adopt it, as it often sounds frivolous and pointless.

A kettle typically consumes 1,200 watts minimum. By reducing the amount of time, it is switched (not the number of times) noticeable power savings are made and will pay for itself over and over. Do not wait until your old kettle fail either. In the meantime, you are losing money daily and so keeping an older inefficient kettle becomes a false economy.

Another form of kettle is shown below, a Thermal Hot Water Dispenser. It can hold a daily consumption of hot water. It boils once in around 20 minutes and then keeps it warm with a top up on just 2 watts. It has a timer to set for boil then it can be set at a minimum chosen temperature; 90f should suffice. This saves time as well as power.

Free Energy

If you want to go mad, it is possible to experience an extreme form super scrimping. As long as the sun is out any time of the year, it is possible to harness its energy and focus it to a small concentrated spot on a kettle. Within minutes, it will be boiling away as if it was plugged in to your mains or on your stove. This is an old satellite dish covered with Infrared reflecting foil. It does good toast & soup too.

Outbuildings

Outbuildings include garages, greenhouses, sheds, workshops and barns. Many of these require power from the mains. The greenest and cheapest alternative is moving completely over to solar power after an energy efficiency makeover. By lowering the power consumption, you lower the power supply required; regarding solar PV systems, the set-up cost is reduced dramatically.

Solar Panel for Garage lighting and charging station

Panels for powering a workshop.

Clean panels at least once a year to keep the efficiency high. Our window cleaner charges £20, but the extra power produced makes up for that within a week or two.

Chapter 15   The Water Bill

This is normally the smallest out of three utility bills. Savings do not normally have an immediate impact either so I have left this last but should not be ignored.

If your property is not on a water meter then consider applying for one. To calculate whether a saving is made or not just compare the number of people living in your property to the number of bedrooms. If there are just two of you in a four-bedroom house then you are being charged for four people; it will be best to apply for a meter. If five people are in a three-bedroom house, then it is best to leave it that way and not have a meter for as long as possible. Although it is the aim of the Water Board to have all properties in the UK metered eventually.

Toilet & Bath

Place (not drop) a brick in the bottom of the cistern. The volume of water used in each flush will be reduced by around 1/8th and save roughly £10 a year on your bill if metered. A water-filled bag sometimes will do the same but as the bag floats around, it can sometimes restrict the internal mechanisms; a brick lying at the bottom in a corner will not.

A bath alert gadget is an alarm that sounds when the bath water reaches the desired depth. This saves on water as it avoids overfilling each time. As it is being filled with hot water via a boiler, it saves on gas and electricity too. This simple £12ish device will pay for itself repeatedly. Search for 'Bath Alarm' or 'Bath Alert' on the internet.

A dripping tap can cost £20 or more a year. After a snap inspection of our home, I found one such tap and a dripping toilet cistern. After repairing both, our water bill dropped by £48 a year.

If you feel confident, carry out simple repairs yourself. Follow a DIY guide such as Readers Digest Energy Efficient Home Manual or look for tips on YouTube. An honest plumber should only charge a few tens of pounds for such jobs; the parts cost pennies. Do get a quote first. Better still, you may have a friend that could do it as a favour.

Chapter 16   Insurances

Dealing with insurances is not the most exciting time you can have, but the savings can be high compared to the time invested. If three hours are spent on this issue and you end up saving £300 a year then you have been working for £100 an hour. Does that sound more exciting? Perhaps you would rather spend two hrs making a pot of home-made Jam (Jelly; USA) to save 50p. You have worked for 25p an hour. So do try and get excited about Insurances.

Vehicle Insurance

If you drive, then do use a comparison website. We use www.gocompare.com . The TV commercials are rather annoying but do the trick. If a company advertises that they are not on comparison websites, it may be because they cannot compete.

Filling in all your details of vehicle model, your personal info, driving history etc takes time but only needs doing once. Filling out one form on a comparison website is far better use of your time than doing it for every company that is not on them. If you do change insurance company, after two years or so they may just increase the premium simply because you are an established customer and take your business for granted. That is the time to change again. As your details are remembered on Go Compare or a similar site, then this does not take long.

Car Hire Insurance

We book a car hire independently from the airline. We use Alamo car hire, and do not accept their insurance. Instead, we use www.moneymaxim.co.uk. The policy covers us for the year on any number of trips, full cover, and is a fraction of the cost offered by the car hire company or the Airline.

Home Insurance

You may have an 'unlimited limit' home insurance. Change this immediately. A home may be worth £250,000 but may only cost around £60,000 to rebuild it from scratch. Again, use a comparison website. I use www.gocompare.com for all such searches simply because it is so much easier keeping all your details in one place. This saves time and effort.

Once you register with a user name and password with such a website, your details are remembered and you can change an insurance provider, energy tariff, pet insurance etc in just a few minutes. If you are not online, ask for help from someone who is. You could save hundreds of pounds a year with just two hours or so of your time. Gather all your existing insurance documents first for direct reference. (We do not have shares in Go Compare in case you are wondering).

To discover how much it would cost to rebuild your home use www.abi.org.uk

Useless Insurance

ID protection insurance is a perfect example. The credit and debit card protection really is not necessary as you are covered by your bank when you become a victim of fraud.

Another useless policy for many is mobile phone insurance. That is because home contents insurance plans can usually be extended to cover the eventuality of your phone being nicked, lost or damaged even when you are away from home. There is no point paying more for a standalone policy.

Chapter 17   Personal Security & Health

As well as financial & health burdens that cause worry, there is always the issue of your property being broken into or your ID used for criminal purposes. It may seem unrelated to relieving a debt problem but the extra anxiety can send people into a lower state of depression. Any actual breech of your personal security can leave a very negative scar on your memories. Therefore, it is a good idea to take a few extra steps with little effort this worry can be minimised. A whole book could be written on this alone.

Security

When out shopping, only take one or two cards with you and note their details separate from the cards; emergency phone numbers against the card numbers for stopping them if lost or stolen. Keep the rest at home hidden.

Use good quality padlocks on any sheds, garage etc. eBay has them for just around £2.50 each, a shop will normally charge around £8.

Leave an LED light on when you go out at night. A 2.5-watt LED light is bright enough to give the impression somebody is in and hardly cost anything to run.

If you cannot afford real CCTV system, just put up a couple of fake cameras with large CCTV signage as a warning. Most thieves will just go elsewhere just in case. Once your debts lower, then consider a real system, £250 should cover a two-camera system.

If you shop online often, ensure you have a full security package such as Kaspersky or AVG to avoid others reading your passwords and account details.

Such steps are small but can help put your mind more at ease and concentrate on paying off debts instead.

Health

It can take several years to pay off your debts. The whole accumulation of a serious credit problem that may take years to solve can take its toll on your health. It can cause headaches, sickness, lack of quality sleep and metal stress in various forms. This can result in time off work, extra family pressures and then perhaps a lower income. This situation will make your position even worse and can end in disastrous scenes.

I am not a doctor or a health expert in any form, but here are a few tips from medical experts and shortened the advice on a few points to save you the time.

Addressing the financial burden in an active way is the first step to recovery; do not just think about it. However, during this process you do need to keep as healthy as possible to remain in control. Obviously, everybody is different, I can only generalise a few points. Nevertheless, if these results' in saving you a few days off work, or help you to have a few extra good quality night's sleep, then this chapter was worth writing.

Bacteria & Germs

Go into a pound store / dollar general store and purchase several small bottles of Anti-bacterial sanitising hand gel. Put one in your car, work desk, toilet etc. Under a stressful situation your natural immunity to colds etc lowers and your body is more susceptible to everyday illnesses; more time off creating even more stress. Reduce this to a lower level. Ensure your home and car is regularly cleaned to reduce the same risk.

Headaches

Many people suffer from intense headaches when the realisation of a serious debt problem emerges. These can go on day after day for months. During the dull and short winter days, a lack of exposure to sunlight can lower resistance to stress related headaches too. A natural reaction is to take the usual medication for fast relief as often advertised on TV. On a long-term basis, this can cause more serious internal damage; I am not a doctor so I will not try to go into detail here. A more natural and zero harmful method is to take a daily Vitamin D tablet. These are very cheap and have other health benefits too. Purchase them from any chemist or even eBay.

Sleep

Simply allow plenty of time for sleep. Lack of it for even two to four days easily cause extra headaches and lack on concentration for work etc. That alone can put a job at risk and increase pressure further. Try not to use alcohol (especially wine) to help you drop off faster, it dehydrates your body during the night and causes a lower quality rest. If you feel you have to have a tipple in order to wind down more quickly, try a liqueur instead.

Best solution of all I found is *Camomile Tea*. It is free from Alcohol, Caffeine and Sugar. It has a very calming effect that takes place almost immediately and last all night. In addition, it is only around 3p per cup. Purchase in bulk if you can to cut it down to 2p.

Alcohol

If you enjoy the odd tipple as I do, then avoid all alcohol for two consecutive days a week. Do not cheat and drink extra on the other five days. This saves a little money and allows your liver to recover and rest before the next drowning.

Sugar

Set one regular day a week where hardly any sugar is eaten. That is not an easy task. (Unless you have a medical condition that requires it). Include foods such as Porridge (Quaker has lowest sugar content), Beans, Toast and plenty of Veg, water or any genuine sugar free drinks. Tea is sugar free but be careful with other drinks, check the package first and be honest with yourself. Cutting the risk of Diabetes is a good idea regardless of any financial situation. As of 2015, the NHS spends 20% of its entire national budget dealing with Diabetes. If this alone were reduced, more funds would be available for research into new treatments & cures for everything else.

Dentistry

I am trying not to make this obvious or sound like your Mum, but looking after your teeth properly will inevitably reduce your annual bills further. Much work done by a dentist could have been prevented. Use mouthwash etc. to help. Who wants to visit a dentist more often than you need to anyway?

Detoxing

To detoxify your body… well it does it naturally. Many products are sold in this field, save your money and just do not bother. Some may accelerate the process a little but that is it. Evidence does show that even a strong cup of tea will have the same effect as some of the products seen in health stores. Just leave the tea bag in for longer and swirl it around; this action is Free!

Some of these tips may sound frivolous, but looking after your health keeps your body in full working order as best as you can; this allows you to keep your income and motivation up. By keeping a check on all your outgoing expenses too, shows how much of it could be lowered or even zeroed with a little thought and effort. These savings can all be transferred to your debts and pull back your debt free date further.

Chapter 18 Shopping

We all like to shop. Perhaps it's excessive shopping that accumulated your debts in the first place. Mine occurred because I purchased a larger house that needed more improvements than I expected. At the same time my business required new equipment and van. I did not super scrimp on any of these purchases; the borrowing got out of hand. I became over confident and simply paid too much for each item. After paying out thousands of pounds to complete these tasks, a holiday, new carpets and furniture did not seem too much of an extra big deal, so we had those too.

After my physical collapse in 2006, I knew we had made a mistake and had to change our ways or become bankrupt. I was constantly offered new credit cards, loans from many sources; it became too easy to keep the spending up at full speed and lose control.

With our home extension, we were charged £450 just to get shot of rubble. I had an estate car sitting outside; I should have made ten trips to the recycling centre and disposed of it myself. It would have taken around ten hours of my time, but that is a £45 an hour saving. My replacement van cost £8,500, I should have searched the classified adverts and got one three years older and paid just £3,000 or so. We could have made the same improvements but with a much lower outlay. These two mistakes alone cost me a year of my life paying back the extra money borrowed.

Such an outlook should filter down into everyday shopping for small items, not just large. This could become a book in itself, but websites such as www.moneysavingexpert.com keep up to date with ever changing offers and ideas whereas a book like this cannot.

eBay

If you are online and you have not registered already, I do strongly recommend eBay or similar. If you are not online or do not wish to register with it, I guarantee you will know someone who is. If you mention to that friend, you need something specific, I am sure they will help you. This in turn actually does them a favour. With every purchase they make without hassle, they increase their *'feedback'* score. Therefore, if they want to sell anything, it makes a potential purchaser more at ease as they can see a higher score than they normally would. So do not feel awkward about approaching someone for such help as you are doing him or her a favour by boosting up personal feedback.

Supermarkets

Consider using Aldi and Lidl supermarkets if you have not already done so already.

When shopping for anything at all, do consider if you really need it now it if you just want it. If you really do need something but can wait, then do so or at least get it cheaper somewhere else. If you just want it, then wait as long as you can then try to get the same item as cheap as possible. Continuing your progress at paying off debts is crucial. This kind of decision-making is important even when you are debt free in order to stay that way. Most millionaires think like this too.

Chapter 19   Bulk Purchasing

Many items that are in your everyday shopping can be purchased in bulk. This saves money and time in future trips to the stores. Begin by setting aside some shelves, a cupboard or space in a garage etc. Nevertheless, do not be tempted to consume more at a faster rate; your saving efforts would be wiped out.

Bulk purchases come it two forms; larger packages of a substance or many purchases of the same to taking advantage of a discount price. Once such items are obtained, try not to be wasteful, this will defeat the object. Beware of items that may have a used-by date. It will be false economy to purchase 10 gallons of milk if it is only going to last a few days. Tea bags last for many months; seek out boxes of 300 or more rather than just 80 or so; just have a think before purchase.

Do work out the maths of price against volume or net weight. Some bulk purchases are more expensive than the smaller volume offers. Some deals like these are genuine mistakes; others are genuinely misleading the consumer.

Tea bags can be purchased 1100 at a time for £9.99 that is £0.009 each. If the same change is made for say 20 different items, then around £600 can be shaved off your shopping bill a year. This is equal to perhaps taking an extra month per year off your debts without any increase in your income, working extra hours or cutting back on your consumption. A 7-yr repayment plan will be cut to 6yrs 5 months when interest saving is taken into account too.

A 12.5kg bag of bird seed at £8.99 can last 4 months. Purchasing smaller bags weekly is far more expensive and time consuming. This single item change in my shopping habit saved approximately £30 a year.

Several hundred pounds extra every year is now transferred to your debts. Always calculate the total saving per year rather than per purchase, then add on a chunk extra in saving due to interest that would otherwise pile up. This single alteration in your shopping habit can pull your final debt free date forward by several months.

Chapter 20   Banking

It is important to address every single outgoing regular charge to your income. It is often drained away to leave you broke, in debt, feeling helpless in a world of greed. Services that are provided for us should be paid for, that I understand; this includes banking services. But as deposits are made into our bank accounts, these funds are used by the bank to lend out to other customers and charge them tens of times higher than the amount they pay out in interest to you (in many cases they don't pay you anything). This difference is added to the banks' profit. Therefore, they are already making money out of your money <u>before</u> you are charged monthly for your account. If you have a credit card with them, they are already making money out of you with that too (well they should not be if you followed chapter 9; do not feel sorry for them).

Banking rules have changed in our favour here. Seven days is the new target in the UK to transfer an existing account to a new one. If you are charged for your banking services each month, then do shop around for a personal 'Classic' bank account. No charges are made at all providing you stay in credit. (Lloyds has one). If your existing bank provides one but you have a charged account and you are 'happy' with the bank; then ask for a new account under the disguise of an eBay shop or a similar reason. Just mention you wish to carry out a small-scale online shop as an example and you want to keep related transactions separate from your personal bills for tax purposes.

Then once opened, transfer all your related Direct Debits to your new account one by one; I very much doubt that the bank will do this for you in this instance. Once this operation is complete, close the previous account. It does take some effort but could save you around £200 a year; transfer this to your debts. Just think in five years, that's £1000 saved, enough for a flight to Las Vegas in peak season for nothing when you are debt free. Where would you rather have your money end up?

If this book has been acted upon in the order advised, by now you should be seeing a large improvement in your finances. Reducing your bank charges to zero is another part of reclaiming your income for your use and not someone else who could not care less about your situation. Do not feel guilty about this action; or any other mentioned in the book for that matter.

Chapter 21   Eco Driving

If you run a car, then obviously reducing expenditure here will free up more funds for your repayment plan. This can be achieved in many ways depending upon how far you wish to go. I will keep to a simple listing so you can refer to it more quickly. Much of this has been widely mentioned in other sources but you may find it handy to keep all such tips in one place such as this. Forming good spending and saving habits can save a fortune even after your full financial recovery. Some millionaires are in the position they are in due to a lifetime of cautious spending.

Fuel Purchasing

Find a local garage that constantly supplies cheaper fuel than most and stick to it. You should know of its opening times, best time to fill when it is less busy etc. This will save you hunting around other towns getting desperate and sometimes pay above your normal price. Always check fuel level before any journey to ensure a return trip without filling at a new garage that may charge an extra £2 or so a tank. If you get desperate and have no other choice, just put in enough to get to a cheaper garage or home plus a bit more. Avoid motorway services unless you risk running dry off course. If you take the precaution mentioned here, this should never happen.

Use a cash-back related credit or debit card. You are going to buy the fuel anyway so this is a good idea. Point cards such as Nectar are usually only offered by garages that are a little more expensive anyway such as BP, so the gain rarely outweighs the cost. Just be careful about how much each point is truly worth. Many point-based offers are worth between 0.1 to 0.5p each. Cash-back rewards are usually many times higher and do not restrict what garage you can use. You can then gain from cheaper fuel plus a few pennies cash-back each time it's used.

Tyres *(Tires; USA)*

Check tyre pressures weekly. Under-inflated tyres cause extra wear to it as well as reduce your fuel economy. Check the tread. Illegal tyres are a danger to you and others as well as risking a fine and points on your license.

Lubricant

Add Slick 50 (a lubricant invented for NASA on the Voyager probes) to the oil sump next time it is changed before the fresh oil is added. This will lengthen engine lifespan by thousands of miles and will last 50,000 miles of driving before another top-up is required during another oil change. Potentially it can save hundreds of pounds in repairs or even a new engine as the mileage clocks up. For just £25 or so, it could lengthen the lifespan of an engine by 2yrs.

Water Protection

Polish the vehicle at least 4 times a year to slow down the advancement of rust. So many more vehicles are scrapped due to bodywork failure rather than mechanical. Ensure the underside is protected from advanced decay via a rust proofing agent such as Wax Oil, (get a garage to do this if you need to; it can be done cheaply, it does not take long; do not get ripped off).

Use WD40 spray (another NASA invention; for the Atlas rocket) on locks, door mechanisms, spray on any exposed cables, spark plugs and fuse casings under the bonnet several times a year. This will repel water spray from the road and help prevent short circuits, engine cut-outs etc.

Washing

Do not use any commercial vehicle washing facilities. Wash your vehicle(s) often yourself to slow down the rust. Try to use rainwater, which is zero cost from your pocket and purer. No water, gas or electric expense; 10p worth of car wash or washing up liquid instead of £10 or so.

Engine Speed

If you have a rev counter on the dashboard, keep your revs below 2,500rpm whilst cruising. Any higher is uneconomical. Drive no faster than 60mph on the motorway / freeway; the national speed limit should be reduced to 60mph anyway for Climate Change reasons. Accelerate and decelerate gently. For slowing, take your foot off the gas before you normally need to and let the air slow you down for a while first for free; it saves wear and tear on your brakes as well as fuel.

As of 2025, I now use a 6-speed van. I can cruise along at 70mph on less than 2000revs per minute giving around 50 miles per gallon.

Weight and drag

Take out any unnecessary weight from your vehicle. Take off roof bars if you have them but hardly use them. Do not drive with windows open on both sides at once on a long journey. The through draught creates enormous drag that will cost extra fuel.

Vehicle Purchase

If you are considering a new vehicle, please try to take out the emotion of what you want and replace it with what you need. Taking into account decreasing value with age, the best age of vehicle at purchase should be between 3-9yrs old. Anything newer will loose value too rapidly, anything much older may have technical problems with possible oil leaks, failing seals, pumps etc and will cost more to run in repairs. You could be lucky if you know the seller / history of the vehicle and get away with something a little older; hence cheaper still.

Does your old vehicle really need replacing? Sometimes spending a little money on it and a good polish inside and out can make it feel like a new car. Sometimes it is best to keep the devil you know rather than the devil you do not know. Other times it really is best to right-off your loss and get something cheaper to run. I always keep a vehicle until it is ready for the scrap yard. Every situation is different. Have a good careful think about that one and do not just assume you need a change because you fancy it; again, that would be an emotional decision. Try to ignore it and examine the numbers only... fuel economy, repairs, devaluation, insurance etc.

Calculate a rough guide price of how cheap a vehicle is to purchase

Start with the purchase price and divide it by the number of years you hope to keep it. When I purchase a 8-year-old van at say £2,500 and keep it for 4 years before scrapping, that works out to just £625 a year. If I bought a much newer van at say £9,000, I would normally keep it for 7 years; it would cost £1,285 a year. A newer van would not improve the service that I give, but the older van will improve my profit margin: more money available to throw at the debts.

Regarding a business, tax relief is available for vehicles but the gain is the tax percentage only. If it is only 20% and yet purchasing an older vehicle gains 50% on direct purchase cost as in the example above, then your decision is not rocket science.

Please do not get too hung up on mileage. A modern engine, if treated well, should last 200,000 miles. I rarely scrapped a vehicle with less. The bodywork requires attention as soon as a purchase is made. Regular washing and polishing is just as important as a service. Do not forget Slick 50 for the engine. It can reduce wear and tear to virtually zero and expand the life of the vehicle.

Early Lesson Learned...

As a youngster, I had the usual desire to own a sports car. In 1987, I did settle on one and yes, it did work with the girls but should not. After around 18 months, I had a small prang and the insurance premium shot up to more than double. It was a shock. This was the first time I took all my personal desires out of the equation and just looked at figures. I sold the car, got myself an old banger (Datsun Cherry -16yrs old if I remember correctly), cost me £300 but was in almost perfect working order. It just had a worn tappet and it sounded like a sewing machine. It was big enough for what I wanted but certainly was not flash. I had it for three years; cheap on insurance, fuel and never broke down. Dividing the purchase price against the time I had it worked out to £100 a year. My finances recovered and allowed me to save for a massive trip around the USA for five weeks covering 12,000 miles. I guess this was the first time I had experienced that such cold financial reasoning can reward you in many unexpected ways.

Frosty Nights

It may sound rather frivolous at first, but if frost is predicted for the night, use some newspapers or an old towel under the wipers to keep it off. This saves time and using a de-icer in the morning. No chemical emissions, energy production, carbon footprint, or cost. We read two-day-old papers from a neighbour instead of her throwing it away or buying our own. They are all recycled afterwards. An estimated saving of around £30 a year on de-icer, more still on newspapers. All the savings go on the debts. (The Christmas lights are all LEDs; they take no more than 40 watts... around 0.76p / 1.3 US Cents per hour. I can afford that. Super scrimping is not about going without anything, but just doing the same as before but at a lower cost).

Satellite Navigation *(Street Pilot or GPS; USA)*

Satnavs are fantastic, even essential if many journeys are made to new towns where a driver may not be familiar. It saves fuel, time and stress. Only purchase models with unlimited free Map Updates. Soon this option will be standard. Set the map options to 'Economical.'

Do beware; such updates via Garmin for instance only work via the latest Windows 10 or 11 operating system. They claim to have the right to discontinue support for any operating system at any time and it only applies to the one Satnav (GPS / Street pilot) module you have purchased. Once it breaks down, that is the end of the 'lifetime maps.' So its lifetime maps with severe restrictions.

At each shopping town, search for the cheapest car park, or free parking facility if you can and save it on the Satnav for future reference. If it has an Eco drive facility, punch in the settings it asks for and turn it on. This will give a constant reading of how economical your driving is taking into account speed, acceleration & braking.

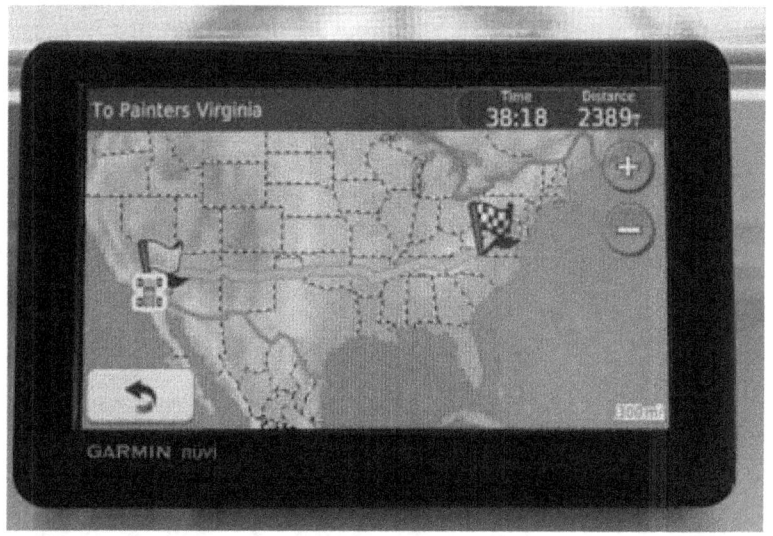

A SatNav / Street Pilot / GPS can show the most economical route regardless of how far it is. As a bonus, it gives accurate driving times. Stops for meals, hotels etc. can be planned instead of being stuck in the middle of nowhere at 2am.

LPG (Autogas)
Liquid Petroleum Gas is a very green form of fuel. However, if you think you will save money, as it is half price of petrol or diesel, think again. The energy content of LPG is 50% that of other fuels. Therefore, the mileage obtained per gallon is also half. Not a single penny will be saved.

Also the fuel 'bits' on the vehicle are more specialised. The spark plugs are four times more expensive and the exhausts (mufflers) are twice that of standard parts on other vehicles. Anything else fails will always require a specialist; a higher hourly charge.

Parking

Almost every town now charges for parking. Norwich, Coventry, Bristol are way above average in parking charges. For the best deals, we sometimes use www.parkopedia.co.uk. If we manage to find a free parking place in a side road not too far the town centre, we mark it as a favourite on the Satnav or map for future reference.

Do also consider using www.parkatmyhouse.com . People have registered their own driveways for parking. These are low cost offers near town centres, railway stations etc. As they are associated with a house, it can be considered as being a secure site rather than a back street public car park. Perhaps you may have a driveway that you could rent out; more about that in Section 3 of this book.

Chapter 22   Computers

This chapter is tricky to write. The need for having a computer or other similar devices vary widely. I can therefore only generalise.

The main rule to follow is never use the very latest version of any purchased program unless you need it for work purposes. The only other exception is Anti-virus / security programs. It certainly would be false economy to scrimp out on security to save £20 and then become a victim of a hacker that empties your bank account.

Free anti-virus programs are available, just 'Google' your search but do look up the feedback by others before downloading one.

Of those that are commercially available, we have tried Norton, McAfee and AVG. The program we now use is Kaspersky. It seems to be most comprehensive and works silently in the background without slowing your machine too much and very few annoying pop-ups.

Old machines

If your old computer(s) that are so slow they cannot run Windows 10 or 11, then don't throw them out. They may not be viable for operating on the Internet, but they have other uses.

Many programs are not recognised by the Windows 10 or 11 operating system. For several years, I have used a photo suite called Roxio 7. Many sections of it have taken a very long time to take full advantage. It cost £70 in 2007 and came with a lifetime licence. To me a lifetime licence means just that. Unfortunately, lifetime to software companies mean – as long as your operating system will run it. This is not stated anywhere.
When we were forced to upgrade from Win 7 to 10 in January 2020, Roxio as well as other programs were not recognised. The obvious option was to pay for the latest versions; a total of £480.

We had an older machine that was not required to be connected to the Internet. It ran Win 7 happily and dedicated it to these 'obsolete' programs. It not only saved money, it also saved many hours learning new forms of software that I did not even need.

Our accounts package is Quicken 2000. As our turnover is just below the VAT limit, that program is all we need. I paid £45 for it in 2000, had a 'lifetime' licence and I never purchased a newer version since. As it does not operate at all on Windows 10, the old machine is now in constant use.

We do not use the latest version of Microsoft Office either. For many years, we had Office 2007 but parts of it did not function well on Windows 10. There is a subscription service by Microsoft with the very latest updates. At £6 a month / £72 a year, that was way beyond my principals. I purchased a full version of Office 2016 instead on a well-known auction website. It included a licence for three computers, contained around 90% of every feature that the subscription service provided and unlimited updates - all for £14 and that was it: not a penny more.

If you do not possess an old machine, ask around your friends, they are worthless to most people. Alternately, purchase a used one on eBay or somewhere similar, pay no more than around £50. You will need a monitor and keyboard too, again these items are almost free these days. Bargains or even free machines can be found on 'Shpock.'

Chapter 23   Gambling

There is often the temptation to have a flutter on the Lottery or on the horses etc to try to get out of debt fast. There are sometimes stories in the press of people who are lucky enough to have had this come true. I know of someone who, after a messy divorce decided to blow the last £3,000 he had to his name on a wild trip to Las Vegas. He ended up winning $1.1 million on a slot machine. At least this person had no debts, just wanted some fun and decided to make a fresh start after his return. He certainly did that, but had already accepted beforehand that he was not going to win a penny. (His ex-wife tried to get her hands on the winnings too; she failed as it occurred after the divorce was finalised).

Perhaps a couple of lines on the lottery is okay for morale, but do accept that it is not going to happen. Keep this kind of fun to a minimum, zero preferably. Treat yourself by popping into the bank and pay another few quid off a loan or credit card instead. At least you will definitely gain this way and not just a massive maybe of one chance in fourteen million. However, if by any chance you do win, I am your best friend.

Chapter 24   Travelling

We all need to take a break to remain sane. This can be looked upon as a reward for renewed effort in a different method of handling finances. Don't be tempted to arrange a holiday costing perhaps £500 after lowering your debts by £300. Hold back until debts have dropped by at least five times the cost of the planned trip. This would then be classed a well-deserved reward without feeling guilty.

Our favourite place to visit in the UK is the Isle of Wight. We always book a caravan, off peak, that is also on a bus route. We always ensure there is a food outlet within walking distance. After several experiments, we have settled on a place based at Sandown Airport. The owners are very flexible regarding dates and price. A bus stop is 200 metres away; a Morrison's and Liddle store (as well as a cheap pub) is less than 500 metres away. The site offers all our scrimping requirements.

The island offers many walking tours; these often include spectacular coastal cliff views. We avoid paying out for most attractions, but do make an exception every so often as a treat and to assist with the island's economy.

USA

Once we became closer to our debt-free position, we began travelling to the USA again twice a year. We book early, used air miles, and always phoned for the best deal.

We book a car hire independently from the airline. We use Alamo car hire, and do not accept their insurance. Instead we use www.moneymaxim.co.uk. The policy covers us for the year on any number of trips, full cover, and is a fraction of the cost offered by the car hire company or the Airline. As a result we can afford a larger vehicle, safer and far more comfortable for long journeys across deserts.

We plan for visiting free attractions such as State Capitol Buildings, open parks, canyons etc. Three quarters of the National Parks in the USA have no entry fees, and at the time of writing 309 are free. There are donation boxes inside the visitor center, where people can put a donation only if they wish to. We thoroughly recommend the Great Smoky Mountains National Park and Canyon de Chelly in Arizona, as both are very beautiful and free of charge!

We do allow for low-cost attractions but put an upper limit of $12 each person. We are very selective with hotels and gained many lessons on obtaining the best deals. After many such trips, we felt qualified to write a book on our low budget touring... Budget Travel USA. All our books are available via www.outerspacebooks.com.

Section Three; Increasing Income without working harder

So far, this book has covered decreasing your debts and developing new spending or rather non-spending habits. The bad news is that regardless of how much you may reduce your outgoing funds as described in Section 2, it can never reach zero. The good news is that the amount you owe as defined in Section One is finite and the extra amount you could obtain in the future is theoretically limitless… but do keep it legal; i.e. without wearing a mask and walking into a bank (even though they are quite prepared to steal from us).

Increasing your income is an important part of the formula in starting a new life without so much worry. I have just touched on a few ideas large and small in this section that your bank would rarely help or advice. They will just encourage you to add to an ISA account, give you a measly 1% interest a year if you are lucky: while they lend it out, and steal 18% or so from another unfortunate customer.

Chapter 25   Rent it out!

Rent out a Driveway

If you live fairly close to a railway station or a town centre, and have a driveway, do consider using www.parkatmyhouse.com . People register their own driveway for parking. If the local charges are say £6 a day, then offer your driveway for £4 a day. In a year, you could be earning over £1000 without lifting a finger. You do not need a PHD, just spare driveway capacity. We knew someone in Greenwich who did this, she had no car at all, and she even rented the property, she did not own it. She asked the property owner permission, as she would then be able to afford her rent more easily, he gladly accepted. She had enough room for two vehicles 7 days a week and earned around £3000 a year. It covered almost half her annual rent.

Rent out a Garage

If you have a garage on your property but do not use it much, then have a serious clear-out. Register with www.storemates.co.uk and list your garage as storage space for someone that needs it. You could earn up to £1000 a year without working.

Rent out a Room

In the UK, a room could be rented out and earn up to £4,250 a year tax-free. If you earn less than your tax threshold, you can have this income without doing anything else. If you pay tax, then you would need to fill in a simple Tax Return to have this extra income tax free. It only takes a few minutes.

Chapter 26   Unwanted Clutter

Over the years, we all accumulate stuff that we never really use any longer or did not need in the first place. The volume can literally give us a headache looking at it all and contemplating sorting it out. Some can be ditched as rotten trash that is not any good to anyone. However, other items may still hold some value and can be sold. Such extra raised funds should be placed on your debts; prioritise as advised in Section 1.

Go through your property one small step at a time. Perhaps you may wish to start with an area that is used the least. It could be a shed, garage or spare bedroom. Dedicate some floor space for sorting. Empty out one draw and then act in a military fashion...

Make separate piles;

1) You need
2) You trash
3) To be recycled
4) To be given away
5) To be sold.

Put back in the draw everything in pile 1. Then repeat with another draw, shelf or cupboard. It does not take long to complete a whole room. Trash everything in Pile 2 straight away. Deal with pile 3 & 4 within hours / days or it will end back in the draws. Pile 5 is your little gold mine.

Pile 5 can be sold via a boot fair (meet swap) ebay or similar. It just depends on what the items are, how many, time available, computing skills etc.

Repeat the same process as you get time. Be thorough and do not kid yourself that a hardened pot of 10yr old paint may come in handy one day. It will not even match anything after 10yrs of discolouration anyway.

This process may sound a little trivial at first but it does have several advantages.

It reminds you what items you already have to reduce future purchases.

Makes more room; reduces the need to buy extra storage space.

Acting green.

Save other people a little money or give them a little more happiness.

Raises funds to pull forward your debt free date.

Declutters your home and your mind.

After decluttering my garage in April 2020, all this wood and a spare roll of roofing felt was converted into five hedgehog houses. They only took around four hours each to construct. I arranged for pick-up only. They were sold for £50 each. The only extra purchase was a bag of clout nails at £4. Total profit from waste products - £246.

Chapter 27   Future Investments

Upon solving a major financial problem, keeping out of debt for life is a major priority. If you feel you have mastered that too, then you may be ready for investing in order to make up for lost time. By putting trust, back into a bank may not be your idea of investing. They may offer a crummy 1- 5% return on any deposits you may make. This hardly even keeps up with inflation. Even with a secure ISA account, you will lose money, as the interest rate gained is currently less than inflation itself. You put £1000 in and next year the figure is £1010 but it is actually worth <u>£980</u> in purchasing power when set against 3% inflation as an example. Always remember the inflation factor as it eats away into your valuations.

So what can we do to make up for lost time & money? We need to look for investments that can give more a year than inflation. Compounding investments for several years can build up to an impressive lump sum. All investments are subject to risk. Even property and pension funds can go down in value as well as up as we have witnessed during the past 30yrs. All I can really do in this area is suggest some ideas for research.

Antiques

These can include furniture, paintings, photographs, jewellery etc. As with any subject, you do have to learn the trade. Specialise in one small area that you may be interested in; it may only take a few weeks of study to secure your first investment. The advice constantly given by antique investors is Buy Quality! Antiques can rise in value by a constant percentage higher than inflation.

Coins & Stamps

Learn from dealer websites but do not necessarily purchase from them. You will get to know what is highly collectable and what is invaluable & common. Then search for the same items elsewhere such as boot fairs, eBay and second-hand shops. Just because an item is old, does not always mean it is valuable. Some Roman coins are only worth around £10, but a 1933 British

Penny is worth thousands – there is only one left to find in the world.

Memorabilia

I have some expertise in this one area. Autographs for example are highly collectable. If you have an interest in a particular subject such as Pop Music, Formula 1, Movie Stars, Football etc then you may wish to collect autographs as an investment. Choose big names (or hedge a bet on upcoming big names) on quality items, if possible, with evidence to show authenticity. Keep them in the dark, and not hang them on the wall. After a little time, your experience grows, contacts build up and bargains begin to surface. Many people have such items in their possession but not know of their true value.

Another advantage with autographs is that they do not take up much room. So small in fact that an entire loose collection can fit inside a safe deposit box in a bank. They only cost around £50 a year and will not require insuring. That is as long as you trust the bank enough for this service. I guess I do, but I keep a record of every item placed in it just in case.

In Dec 2013, I was shown a Neil Armstrong Autograph in a scrapbook of Apollo newspaper clippings in a local museum. My sister-in-law worked there. At first, I offered £100 for an item they did not want to display. After a little faffing around on their part, they gladly settled on £50. It is worth a minimum of £2,500. That is a massive gain of 50 times what I paid out in one day; equal to an investment of 18,250%. per year. My wife obtained a signed book by Carl Sagan for £1 at a charity store but its worth around £300. I do realise it doesn't happen every day, but if a number of such purchases are made, then the money lost while in debt will soon be caught up and exceeded.

Now is a good time to collect silver bullion in the form of coins and silver bars. Silver reached a rock bottom price in 2000 but has been rising steadily since: around 8x more than you would by sticking your money in a bank. Purchase from dealers, not individuals. Be aware that bronze has almost exactly the same weight as silver, so it is easy to cover a bronze item in silver and sell it on as solid silver.

Regaining losses from the past is how many millionaires think. It may not be your aim to become one, it is certainly not mine, but the purpose is to recuperate funds. That in itself could be a worthwhile dream after becoming Debt Free - without a single banker in sight! Sadly, the same cannot be said about recovering lost time. So the sooner you act, the less you waste.

We have set up a wildlife sanctuary, astronomical observatory with another home after purchasing a parcel of 36 acres of land. The same frugal techniques are still used to stretch every penny and make our money work harder. Fast cars and expensive watches do not excite us, but buying land does. Land largely increases in value, but cars and watches generally do not: although there are always exceptions.
www.northstaroasis.co.uk

Write a Book: Some say that there is a book in everyone. To get something published, you have to convince the publisher that sales will be high enough to make it worth their while.

With an E-Book or self-published paperback; a minimum sales estimate is not required. Just write it in a Word Document and submit it to Amazon or similar. It does require conversion, formatting etc. beforehand to a PDF format but Amazon itself can do that now. If you don't feel confident about it as there is a lot to learn, companies are offering this conversion process for a fee of up to £500 but try it yourself first and keep all the royalties rather than sharing. Purchase a book on Self-Publishing; the '… for dummies' series has one.

If you still do not feel confident with the conversion process, ask someone to help you. Amazon will require a minimum of 50% of each sale. It is best if certain guidelines are followed before a single word is written. Royalty payments would be made to you monthly with full proof of sales. Tax matters will be your responsibility. Our biggest seller is on attracting hedgehogs, yes you read it correctly. I published it in 2014, and have made around £7000 in royalties so far. A little time is spent each year with updates, but apart from that, I just watch the pennies flow in monthly. We do have a contact to help with proof reading, layout etc. at very low cost. Feel free to get in touch… www.outerspacebooks.com

Our current situation as of 2025.
Since 1994, I commented an unusual business, a mobile planetarium that I take to schools and colleges around south east England. My fees were almost always met by a school fund in

one form or another and has given me a reasonable income in an occupation that I loved. If I could have offered the service for free, I would have. However, from 2024, the new Labour government has slashed the source of these funds, added VAT on private school tuition fees, and increased National Insurance on every employee - all at once.

Our school bookings dropped away to such a degree that the business became unsustainable. For the first time ever, we had to draw on savings to pay our basic bills. The time had arrived to semi-retire or in time, run the risk of becoming bankrupt.

We purchased a three-bedroom lodge on the Isle of Wight; we just need to pay the ground rent each year. But our main home then became available to put up for sale. All of that fund is tax-free and will be invested in low risk / high(ish) interest accounts. That income together with our book sales ands still operating the planetarium business for just five weeks a year will pay our new lifestyle without touching the main capital. It's a life we didn't expect, but has turned out okay despite the sheer greed from creditors.

Take control as fast as you can...

Good Luck!

Chapter 28   Links for Reference

For Checking your credit score… www.experian.co.uk

For insurances and energy tariffs etc… www.gocompare.com

Updated money saving tips… www.moneysavingexpert.com

Low cost shopping… www.ebay.com

Supermarket Prices… www.mysupermarket.co.uk

Finance Comparison… www.moneysupermarket.com

Rebuild House Calculator… www.abi.org.uk

Low cost parking… www.parkopedia.co.uk /
www.parkatmyhouse.com

Say no to expensive calls… www.saynoto0870.com

Rent out garage space and more… www.storemates.co.uk

Car Hire Insurance… www.moneymaxim.co.uk

These links are found on
www.outerspacebooks.com
Click on the page with this book tittle.

If you have a suggestion to contribute toward further editions of this book…

pbassett2001@gmail.com

Chapter 29 Other books by the Author

New books will be published in the coming years. Refer to
www.outerspacebooks.com for signed copies, updated
listings and direct links. Some have a supporting website.
The following are available…

 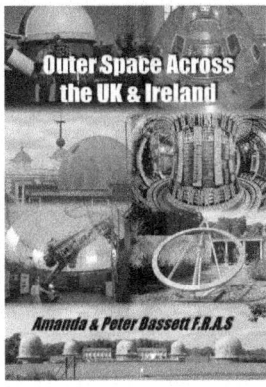 

All book sales support four charities;
Cancer Research UK
Kent Air Ambulance
Smile Malawi Orphanage in Africa
British Hedgehog Preservation Society

www.ingramcontent.com/pod-product-compliance
Lightning Source LLC
Chambersburg PA
CBHW070826180526
45168CB00002B/754